Break the
One-Armed Bandits!

Frank Scoblete

Bonus Books, Inc., Chicago

05 04 03 02 01   12 11 10 9 8

Library of Congress Catalog Card Number: 93-74131

International Standard Book Number: 1-56625-001-3

Bonus Books, Inc.
160 East Illinois Street
Chicago, Illinois 60611

Printed in the United States of America

This book is dedicated to

Carol DeCicco and Fran Applebaum,
who have made my work easier

and
to the usual suspects

my parents, my wife, my sons

Contents

"The greatest task before civilization at present is to make machines what they ought to be, the slaves, instead of the masters of men."
—Havelock Ellis

Introduction

This is a book about machines—machines programmed to take your money—that people have quite rightly dubbed "one-armed bandits." This appellation, given over a hundred years ago, is still the most popular and colorful phrase used to describe them. It is also an anthropomorphic way of looking at them, ascribing to the machines human characteristics and underlying human motivation—in this case, banditry.

In keeping with this point of view, my approach to the slot machines has a human face and a human voice. I have personally interviewed hundreds of people for this book, from players to computer experts to casino personnel to casino executives, and my researchers have interviewed many hundreds more. Whenever feasible in this book, I have let the people themselves do the talking—from experts to eccentrics.

You wouldn't think that a simple machine game—the essentials of which are to put in a coin or coins, pull a handle or press a button, and get a decision before starting the process all over again—would warrant a whole book. But anything people do has levels to it that belie the simplicity of the thing itself. This is as true of the slots as it is true of table games or sporting events or cooking or strolling on a beach. The slot machines, and by extension, the playing of slot machines, only *appear* simple. It is that *appearance* that has led many gamblers to their ruin on these devices. I hope this book will rip away the simple appearance and give you the complicated underlying substance of the playing of these machines.

This book is a first in many ways. It gives a complete background and history of the machines. It gives reasonable explanations for their phenomenal growth and popularity. It explains exactly how the machines work—especially how the modern, computer-driven "smart" machines function—and how they "scientifically" evolved over time. It gives many excellent and original playing and machine-selection methods culled from slot experts and from my own analysis of this book's biggest breakthrough: an insider source's detailed explanation of how "loose" and "tight" machines were placed in a particular casino or casinos. No book, magazine or newspaper article has *ever* had this information—despite the tremendous speculation on the subject—until now.

I would like to thank the many people who have helped me with this project. Thanks to gaming experts Dr. Marvin Karlins and Mr. Jim Hildebrand for allowing me to quote their insights and observations, and for reading and commenting on my manuscript. Thanks to the pseudonymous Mr. Handle, my "Deep Throat," for revealing the casinos' slot machine placement secrets and philosophy. Also, thanks to the many slot industry experts who gave me their insights and opinions but wished to remain anonymous. Thanks to my publisher and editors at Bonus Books for working hard to make our gambling line second-to-none. A special thanks to the many slot players who took the time to talk to me or my researchers. Thanks to my intrepid researchers, Alene Paone, Carol De-Cicco, Albert Ross and Howard T. Mann, without whom this book couldn't have been written.

1

The Allure of the Machines

Circa 1958, Las Vegas.

The flyers, publicity packets and advertisements for the various casinos show smiling, impeccably dressed men and women. The men wear tuxedos or, at the very least, suits and ties, and the women wear gowns or cocktail dresses. If the photo shows a game, it is invariably roulette. More often than not, the photo shows people dining. The feeling generated by these images is one of luxury, money, more money and class.

The billboards around town advertise restaurants, shows, room rates. Rarely is there a billboard for the actual games themselves, and if there is, it is for blackjack ("21") or craps or roulette. And if the billboard photo shows people playing these games—they are men, sometimes with well-dressed, perfectly coiffured women smiling in the background at the good fortune of their husbands or gentlemen friends. If any billboards or advertisements for slots are to be seen, they are usually for downtown gambling joints catering to nickel players and cheap buffet-eaters. (And by nickel here I mean five cents, not five dollars.) In fact, some major casinos have very few slot machines in their main casino areas—some don't have any! Slots, after all, are somewhat unsavory and, yes, somewhat silly.

You pick up a book about gambling, any book of the period, and the assumption is that the men play the table games and the women watch, or, if the women are pesky, they go over to the slot area with a bunch of coins graciously given by their husbands, or gentlemen friends, and there they play the one-armed bandits—for nickels, or, just as often, for pennies. Serious gambling is for men. Serious gambling takes place at the *tables*—where man to man, dealer to player, real money is won or lost.

You see, Las Vegas was built on table games. Fully 80 to 95 percent of a given casino's hold came from players playing at the tables. Table-game players were the lions of Vegas and their action was courted and nurtured. They were the kings of the casinos and everyone catered to their whims.

Slots were an addendum to the main thesis. Slots were for women. Or those not in the know. Or people so down on their luck that they couldn't afford the stakes necessary to play a serious table game. Slot action was *tolerated* but never encouraged in the glamorous casinos of the period. Slot machines were, quite literally, "babe" sitters—as whatever babe a man was with, be she wife or girlfriend or hired gland, had to be amused and entertained while he gambled. The kind of man who played slots would be found in a saloon, not a glamorous casino, more often than not spitting gobs of tobacco juice into a spittoon.

Downtown, it was one-armed bandits played by tooth-less crones and cowless cowboys and the down and outers—the graying, decaying underbelly of gambling civilization. Spit! Toon!

If a "regular" person admitted to playing the slots, it was done shamefacedly: "Oh, I play [*whisper*] *the slots*," as if to admit such a thing was tantamount to screaming at the top of one's lungs: "Look at me, everyone, I'm a BIG IDIOT!" The real gamblers disdained slot players . . . and so did the fancy casinos. Until . . .

Cut to . . .

The Present.

Las Vegas is not the only gambling venue in the country anymore, although it's still the biggest, the best and certainly the brightest. There's Atlantic City and the Mississippi and Colorado riverboats and New Orleans and all those hundreds of Indian reservations across the length and breadth of this great and gambling-hungry nation of ours. Where once there were dozens, now there are hundreds of casinos in Nevada. Where once there were none, there are now hundreds more casinos everywhere else. And the industry is still growing. Mankind has had a stone age, a bronze age, an iron age. Today, in America, it's the gambling age—but it's still involved with metals, the metals of the machine! For the one-armed bandit is now king.

And now when you see the advertisements and brochures and billboards and publicity packets, you see the smiling faces of women and *men!* All playing—the slot machines! Huge billboards proclaim the various types of slot machines available for slot players (Black Gold! Neptune's Treasure! The Fabulous Fifties! and on and on) in denominations of five cents, 25 cents, 50 cents, one dollar, five dollars, all the way to some machines that cost a staggering five hundred dollars to play! Monster progressive jackpots are announced: $10,000,000 Megabucks! $2,000,000 Quartermania! $250,000 Nevada Nickels!

The casinos themselves are jam-packed with machines and filled to overflowing with people of every race, class and credit line playing them. No longer do the glamorous Strip casinos of Las Vegas relegate the machines and their players to the netherworld of gambling's limbo—the outer fringes of their establishments where, like whores, they wait to be filled with coin and yanked about. Today, they are front and center. The first thing you see when you enter today's casinos are rows upon rows of slots. Sparkling, beautiful, proud and greedy slots, just waiting for your action.

The slot player is now the *preferred* player and pictures of jackpot winners adorn the walls of many casinos. Sporting smiles and giant checks that proclaim their wins and flanked by smiling casino executives, the slot players are now kings and queens of casinodom.

Indeed, the table games now account for only about 40 percent of the casino industry's profits. Some gaming experts predict that by the turn of the century fewer than 20 percent of the total industry take will come from table game players. More people than ever before are gambling in casinos in America but the overwhelming majority of them are gambling at the machines. Most gambling floor space is now devoted to slot and video poker machines, with the tables squeezed into the center as opposed to the slots being pushed to the sides.

So what happened? How did the meek and lowly slot machine (and player) inherit the gambling earth? What changed? Why do the casino billboards almost universally tout the paybacks of their machines? Promote their slot clubs? Show pictures of happy slot players? Why is it suddenly okay to be a slot player? And who plays these machines, anyway?

For most casinos, gone are the days of tuxedos and cocktail dresses and table games. Table game areas are fast becoming gambling's Jurassic Parks and table game players are its dinosaurs. The world of the machines is the brave new world and gambling's Luddites cannot destroy the rows and rows of twinkling, jingling, coin-spewing mechanical marvels. The clock cannot be turned back. The slot machine reigns.

I asked Dr. Marvin Karlins, psychologist, novelist and gaming writer, whose excellent gaming column "The Psychological Edge" appears regularly in *WIN Magazine*, to share with me his analysis concerning the growth of the slots and, more importantly, why people play them.

"I think there are three major reasons for the phenomenal growth of machine play in America," states Karlins. "The first has to do with the introduction of the giant jackpots. For a little investment, three dollars, two quarters even, a gambler can win a great deal of money. He can become a millionaire. So there's the lure of the big payout for a small investment. In the old days, the biggest win was a hundred dollars or so. There were no progressive jackpots or linked progressives like Megabucks or Quartermania.

"The second reason has to do with the percentage the house takes from the gambler. Today's machines, particularly in Las Vegas casinos and even Atlantic City, are giving you a better payback. No one really knows what the early machines held back, maybe as much as 50 percent, since casinos were not really regulated as they are now. Today, you have machines paying back anywhere from 88 to 98 percent of what's put in them. So now they are a more decent gamble than they used to be when paybacks might have been around that 50 percent range.

"The third major reason for the increase in machine play has to do with the skill factor. Video poker, for example, gives an expert player a real shot at winning if you know the proper strategies to employ for each type of game."

Of course, the three reasons Karlins outlines are not the only reasons for people playing the machines. As in the past, some individuals prefer the slots, not because of big jackpots or better paybacks, but because it affords them a certain anonymity that table games don't. Karlins states: "The slot machine player is in a non-threatening environment, where his or her decisions will not be second-guessed. There is no embarrassment as there might be at a blackjack table where you make a stupid move and other players get on you. You can also play at your own pace, fast or leisurely."

Personal interviews I conducted with hundreds of slot players tend to substantiate Karlins' ideas. Theresa, a school teacher from California, plays quarter slots because "I can take my time. Nobody is looking at me or bothering me. It's just me and the machine. No dealer is waiting impatiently for me to make a decision. My husband plays blackjack and invariably, when he finishes, he's somewhat angry either because he lost or because of how someone played at his table. I don't have that at the slots. Also, I can play for smaller amounts of money. If I lose, I'm not losing that much. The table games are generally too expensive."

Another factor that is simultaneously both a cause and an effect of the growth in machine play has to do with the sheer variety of machines available for today's players. Walk through any casino's slot area and you'll notice one-coin, two-coin, three-or-more-coin machines; some with fruit symbols, some with bars and stars and faces and places and logos; paying different amounts on different lines; some with linked progressives, in-house linked progressives, individual progressives or all three—in denominations of five cents to five hundred dollars. The slot player today has a veritable supermarket of selection possibilities when entering a casino. And generally the slot player, as in Theresa's example above, has a greater opportunity to play within a gambling "comfort zone" where the stakes do not cause the individual to "sweat it out."

Added to these is the loss of the old stigma that used to be attached to playing the machines. Indeed, slot-play action is lionized by the very casinos that used to scorn it. Slot players are courted, wined and dined just the way table-game players once were. And why not? Obviously, if you are reading this book you are a slot player or, at the very least, interested in playing the slots. Aren't you risking good money to play those machines? Of course. And shouldn't you be treated to the good life, casino style, if your action merits it? Absolutely. The casinos have simply awakened to the fact that slot play is now a mainstay of their enterprise because it gives the small-stakes and large-stakes players alike an affordable, comfortable, non-threatening and enjoyable alternative to table games.

As one casino executive I talked to said, "Gambling has changed. There used to be a small number of casinos competing with one another in one state for the attention of big players—players who would bet thousands or tens of thousands of dollars at the table in a given session. And these players would come from all over the country, since they could afford it, and gamble at the tables—big money was spent. And there were more than enough of these players to go around.

"But now that big money has been spread around. Big players are not enough to sustain today's casinos because there are only so many big players but so many more casinos for them to play in. We now need volume, tremendous volume. Slot machines give us big volume with very little fluctuation in our expectation. When you have thousands of machines, essentially programmed to return a given amount, you get that amount. That's very important to us. It's almost a fixed income."

So slot players and slot and video poker machines are truly the lifeblood of today's casino enterprise. Slot players are the middle class of the casino kingdom, the economic backbone of the nation of chance. Thus, if you pulled the plug on the slots, you would pull the plug on the casino industry as a whole and, like the Roman Empire, it would be laid waste.

Do most slot players realize their importance to the casinos where they play? Strangely and sadly, no. Many slot players are still laboring under the archaic and mistaken notion that their play doesn't really count the way a table-game player's does. Thus, many are not looking to capitalize on their "action" at the slots, action that could very well earn them casino perks (or *comps* = complimentaries).

In a survey I took of 2,000 slot players nationwide, *most* did not belong to a slot club at the casinos where they played (even if the casino aggressively advertised it!), thus most did not realize the extent of the comps available to them based on their play. More startling still, most players had never attempted to find a book on slots (there aren't that many good ones available), understand how the machines worked, or whether there were legitimate winning strategies that could be utilized when approaching slot play.

Joey and his wife, Lorraine, play the slots several times a year in Atlantic City. "We drive down from Philadelphia. We bring a couple of hundred dollars each. It never dawned on me to join a slot club. It was Lorraine's idea. Now, every so often we get comped to a meal in the coffee shop and sometimes we're offered discounts on rooms. We haven't changed how much we play for, these are just extras I never would have thought of."

Joey and Lorraine were representative of the majority of the people I surveyed in another way. There was no rhyme or reason to their play. Stated Lorraine: "I just pick a machine at random and start playing." Did she use some kind of money management scheme to help her in her attack on Lady Luck? "What's money management? I just play until it's time to go or until I've lost everything I brought with me." Joey was the same way. "Don't all the machines pay back the same? I mean, what's the difference if you play one machine or the other?"

Well, the difference could be between winning and losing, or, at worse, between losing a little and losing a lot!

Of course, as in any endeavor, there are remarkably savvy slot players in casinoland. Although they form a distinct minority of the slot players I surveyed (and by assumption the slot-playing public), these players not only understood the basics of how slot machines worked but had methods of play and money management systems, some of which I'll delineate in this book, that were quite astute and based on thousands upon thousands of hours of play. The experienced and savvy slot players all belonged to slot clubs and took advantage of every promotion, every room or meal deal offered.

Slot play is no longer on the rural fringes of the casino landscape. Savvy slot players are accorded the full range of complimentaries and courtesies once accorded only to table-game players. There are free or discounted rooms, shows, special promotions, complimentary meals, tournaments and prizes. The world of the savvy slot player can be every bit as entertaining, challenging and exciting as the world of the table-game player—if you know what you're doing.

The mere fact that you have purchased this book potentially puts you in the ranks of the slot-playing elite. If "knowledge is power" then this book will arm you to the teeth for your assault on the one-armed bandits. It contains viable playing systems and strategies plus money management advice culled from experienced, intelligent, insightful slot players. But more importantly, it gives you never-before-revealed information that will help you *select* which machines are worth playing and which machines should be avoided.

The selection of the machine is the first and, perhaps, the single most important decision a slot player has to make. Unfortunately, though, most players I surveyed never gave a thought as to which machine they would put their hard-earned money into.

And here's another factor that is sometimes overlooked by many gambling writers and slot players alike: Not all machines are created equal. Two seemingly identical machines, sitting side by side, will not necessarily be programmed to pay at the same rate. Some machines are "loose." That is, they pay back a greater percentage of the coins put in them. And some machines are "tight"—they *keep* a greater percentage of the coins played. Seemingly identical machines in the same row, the same carousel, are not all functioning the same way—some may be "loose" and some may be "tight." How machines are placed in a row, in a bank, in a carousel, in a casino is the BIG INDUSTRY SECRET! Individual casinos guard their "loose" and "tight" slot machine distribution information with as much fervor as the government guards the gold at Fort Knox.

Naturally, "loose" and "tight" are relative terms. Comparatively speaking, machines in Atlantic City casinos are tighter than machines in Las Vegas. Atlantic City casinos pay back on average between 88 and 91 percent of the coins put in their machines, whereas Las Vegas' casinos average between 94 and 97 percent on their machines. So does that mean the best, that is to say, the "loosest," machine in Atlantic City will only pay back 91 percent? No. You might have an Atlantic City machine paying back 98 percent in a given Atlantic City casino, comfortably nestled between two machines paying back a mere 86 percent. In Vegas, you might have a 99 percent machine hidden away in a bank of 88 percenters.

On average, Las Vegas has looser machines than does Atlantic City. *On average,* machines in Nevada casinos (but not non-casino venues such as drug stores, laundries, etc.) are looser than machines in other states. However, an Atlantic City, Indian reservation, New Orleans or riverboat slot player, with a little scouting and, yes, a little luck, could very well find himself or herself sitting at a machine looser than the average Las Vegas machine. Thus, the key is to find the loosest machines even in the tightest casinos!

So, are there ways to ferret out these better paying machines?

Yes!

The book you are holding contains solid approaches that you can utilize to increase your possibility of winning; approaches that reflect a profound knowledge of the machines and how they work; and, for the first time ever, an *inside* source's revelation and analysis of the BIG INDUSTRY SECRET—how machines were distributed throughout a particular casino. In short, this book will explain *for the first time ever* how a casino determined where its "loose" and "tight" slots would go. This *insider* information, coupled with the common-sense, logical playing and money management approaches delineated in this book, will go a long way in helping you learn how to break those one-armed bandits and come home with the money!

2

Time Slots

A Brief History of the Slot Machine

I was at a wedding reception recently.
I heard the bride's mother say: "My daughter hit the jackpot by marrying Jason." Later on, a tremendously boring individual regaled our table with tales of his many cars. Finally, he got to his latest: "A real lemon," he stated. "A real lemon."

I heard a woman in her late 70s say to a teenage girl (a girl who was clacking her gum so loudly that it sounded as if she were the percussion part of a band): "Dearie, it is not lady-like to chew gum in public. In fact, ladies never chew gum." The teenager looked at her as if she were from another planet and continued chewing and clacking that gum like a cow.

At another table, I heard someone say: "That job Willie has is a plum." Still another person talked about the "mint" so-and-so made this year in the stock market. And, of course, everyone talked about the bride as being a "peach" of a girl.

What all these individuals had in common, whether they knew it or not, was a vocabulary and/or moral code based on one of the most nefarious yet simultaneously popular mechanical devices ever invented—the slot machine. The terms jackpot, lemon, plum, mint, and peach and, yes, even the social appropriateness of chewing gum by women in public all have their origin in the history and mythology of the slot machine. Indeed, I heard no one say "He won a cigar!" when referring to the good fortune of the groom in marrying the bride, but that is another term directly related to the slot machine. I remember this saying (vaguely) as a kid growing up in Brooklyn. (Although I guess it is a little archaic now in this anti-smoking age.)

The Early Days

The first coin-operated gaming devices were invented on the East Coast in the 1880s, and by 1890 they had spread across the country where they found a ready home in the tumultuous and wide-open city of San Francisco, the city that forevermore would be credited as the cradle of their actual conception, birth and growth.

Situated mostly in saloons and brothels, often in the notorious Barbary Coast and Tenderloin districts, these "nickel in the slots" were mostly poker machines where the player would "win a cigar" or free drinks for getting certain hands. These early slot machines carried an enormous vig ("vig" or "vigorish" is a gambling term for the percentage or tax the house takes out of a player's win; "vig" is also another term for the house edge) since they invariably were missing two cards of different suits between the 10 and the ace. This practice cut in half the number of potential royal flushes a player could get, and the number of cigars the proprietor would have to pay out in the long run. Naturally, the players were unaware of this state of affairs and played blithely on, while the saloons and brothels raked in the enormous profits.

From the saloons and houses of ill-repute, these "slot machines" moved to the cigar stores, soda fountains, sundry stores, bowling alleys and social clubs of the era. To skirt the laws that were loosely enforced about gambling, many of the early slot machines were dubbed "trade stimulators" since they were supposedly used to stimulate a business' trade. However, it was estimated at the time (circa 1890s) that more than 60 percent of the cigar stores in San Francisco, for example, made their *primary* incomes from slots—and not the selling of various tobacco products. The trade the playing of slot machines stimulated was actually more playing of slot machines!

The Father of the Modern Slot Machine

Although there were many slot inventors and manufacturers and types of machines, the individual credited with creating the "modern" slot machine of spinning reels and cash payouts was Charles August Fey, a German immigrant who settled in San Francisco. His "Liberty Bell" slot machines became the standard upon which all future slot machines would be based and judged. Built in San Francisco in 1899, the Liberty Bell had three reels with various card-suit symbols, horseshoes and, of course, liberty bells. The highest payout was accorded to three liberty bells.

So popular was this three-reel design with players and manufacturers alike that the Liberty Bell, now generically known as the "bell" machine, was appropriated and copied by the other slot manufacturers throughout the country. By 1905, bell machines could be found throughout the United States, usually in the cigar stores, bowling alleys, saloons, barber shops and houses of ill-repute. From cowpokes in the West to factory workers in the East, the slot machine was beginning to be the preferred game of chance for the lower classes.

The Liberty Bell (or generic "bell machine") was a simple machine to understand. Each reel operated independently, stopping in a one, two, three order. Each reel had 10 symbols or stops, and thus there were 1,000 different combinations $(10 \times 10 \times 10 = 1,000)$. However, to win the top prize, you would have to line up the three symbols that appeared only once on each reel—in this case the bell. Thus, there was one way to do that $(1 \times 1 \times 1 = 1)$ out of a potential 1,000 three-reel combinations. To this day, the essential mathematics of the slot machines has not changed, although there are now three-, four- and five-reel slots, and reels containing 20 to 25 different symbols or stops. The earliest machines were notoriously "tight" and, quite often, "rigged" to prevent too many big payouts. They were indeed "one-armed bandits."

The Assault Against Loose Living

The first days of the twentieth century saw a backlash developing against these "tight" machines and the "loose" living that they represented. By 1906, from the East Coast to the West Coast, the forces of religion and righteousness were beginning to grow and their voices were beginning to be heard. Pulpits and podiums throughout the land rang with the voices of God's and "good living's" messengers, all telling the rest of society what were worthy and proper pastimes for decent, God-fearing, right-living Americans. Booze and whores and gambling didn't make the cut and thus were singled out as particular examples of the devil's dominion on the earth. The slot machine came in for particular notice, as it represented machine-age science in the service of sin, sloth and Satan.

And then on April 18, 1906, the San Francisco earthquake occurred, and it wiped out the business district and most of the residential community, leaving more than half the city's residents homeless. This earthquake also wiped out every single slot-machine manufacturer in the city! Yet, as San Francisco rebuilt itself from the ashes, so did the slot machine manufacturers and soon they were operating at full steam again.

However, the earthquake did something else again. The pulpit pounders and prophets saw this calamity as a sign that God was fighting on their side and they redoubled their efforts to have the nefarious slots (as well as brothels, saloons, and liquor) banned for all time. In 1909 San Francisco outlawed the slots, in 1910 Nevada followed suit, and in 1911 the California legislature banned slots from the entire state. Still more states eventually banned these "machines of the devil."

Most of San Francisco's slot manufacturers, including Charles Fey, immediately moved their bases of operation to the East, but the Nevada legislature gave them reason to return. In 1912, the state legalized slot machines as trade stimulators, permitting them to be sold, maintained and operated but with one stipulation: They could not pay out cash rewards. And thus the era of the "gum" machine began. It was during this period when slot machines changed their symbols from cards and card suits (obviously a sign of gambling) to fruit—cherries, plums, lemons, oranges, peaches, etc., and the labels of the gum dispensed, which have evolved into the "bars" of today's slot machines.

As long as the patron putting money in the slot machine was given a stick of gum, the machine was technically considered a vending machine and not a gambling device. Although this was a clever ruse to skirt the laws, it could not fool the angry legions of the Lord. Indeed, gum machines were gambling devices since they offered rewards (other than that initial stick of gum) for continued playing. And, of course, the vig was enormous. More horrifying than the house edge was the fact that now even women and children were being lured into playing these infernal devices. And thus, the simple act of chewing gum suddenly gave cause for concern. Where had the gum come from? More often than not, the belly of the metallic beast! And so gum chewing became unladylike and was discouraged.

Prohibition and Slots: I Can't? I Will!

By 1916, the armies of the Lord (and they were legion!), among them the Anti-Saloon League and the Women's Christian Temperance Union, along with individual but high-profile reformers such as Billy Sunday, Pussyfoot Johnson and Carrie Nation were winning their battle against the evils of alcohol, gambling and loose living. On August 1, 1917, the United States Senate passed a resolution to create the 18th Amendment, which would outlaw the manufacturing, distribution, sale and use of alcohol. The amendment became the law of the land on January 16, 1920, having been ratified by every state with the exception of Rhode Island and Connecticut.

With the closing of legal saloons across the nation, the legal use of "gum-vending" slot machines declined, since saloons were the primary establishments that made use of them. But this didn't stop the spread and growth of slots. In fact, Prohibition encouraged them. Tell an American he can't do something and his first inclination is to do it.

Thus, the "Roaring Twenties" saw an explosion in the growth of slot machines. Every speakeasy and "soda parlor" from New York to San Francisco had its lineup of slot machines for its parched patrons to play. It was during this era, dubbed "the Golden Age of Slots" by slot historians (1919–1933), that the slots confirmed their unsavory reputation and were officially dubbed "one-armed bandits" as they were now   inti-mately linked with mobsters from coast to coast who, more often than not, controlled their manufacture and distribution. It was during this era too that "mints" were substituted for gum in the machines because mints had a longer shelf life. Also, many machines were now offering "jackpots" for certain combinations. Indeed, the burgeoning underground economy saw the creation of slot machines that used dimes, quarters and even silver dollars as well as nickels. Slots were starting to become big-time gambling devices and fully one-eighth to one-fourth of a speakeasy's profits would come from their use. Prohibition simply proved an old saw: "Tell me I can't and I will!"

The Continued War Against the Slots

But the Golden Age of slot machines ended with the repeal of Prohibition and the licensing of legal drinking establishments. Unfortunately, while the federal and local governments would now tolerate alcohol consumption, slot machines were still outlawed. Mayor La Guardia of New York personally presided over the dumping of almost 1,200 slot machines into the ocean in 1934. And state and local prosecutors and attorney generals from around the country, among them future Chief Justice of the Supreme Court Earl Warren, at the time District Attorney of Alameda County, California, went the whole nine yards in attempting to ban slot machines and prosecute anyone who bought, sold or used them.

To circumvent this persecution and prosecution, giant gambling ships took to the offshore waters with their payloads of table games and slot machines. Except for Nevada, which had legalized gambling in 1931, the slots were *machina non grata* throughout the United States.

World War II saw an interruption in the sale, manufacture and distribution of slot machines as the slot machine giants—Mills, Bally, Jennings, among others—turned their attentions to the war effort. After the war, slot machine sales skyrocketed as private men's clubs, private golf clubs and various non-profit service and veteran's clubs made use of the money-making power of the slots in the service of "charity." But the slot machine manufacturers were in for a great surprise as this mini-Golden Age soon came to a grinding halt. In 1951, Congress passed the Johnson Act, which banned slot machines in all states without legalized gambling—which meant essentially that slot machines were allowed in Nevada and nowhere else.

The Modern Era

And thus it stood, until the prodigious growth of casino gaming in Nevada caught the attention of the rest of the country. Even so, as stated in chapter one, the slot machine was the poor sister compared to the table games. She was Cinderella before the ministrations of the Fairy Godmother changed her into a sparkling beauty instead of a disheveled domestic. Then two things happened to stimulate the growth of slot play: The rest of the country, starting with Atlantic City, and rapidly followed by Indian reservations, then riverboats and land-based casinos in Mississippi, Colorado, and elsewhere, decided to cash in on Las Vegas' cash cow; and Bally Manufacturing developed an electromechanical machine capable of paying out over 50 different payoff combinations of various sizes in a hopper capable of holding upwards of 2,500 quarters. Added to these features was the multiple-coin-play feature, which revolutionized slot play and made possible the phenomenal growth of casino slot profits. Now, players played three, four and five quarters (instead of one), anticipating greater wins while the casinos reaped greater rewards.

Slot play had now become serious gambling and Bally flooded the market with machines of every denomination and capability—capabilities that included sound effects, video and music. The dollar slot now became the fastest-growing type of machine in the country, as casinos discovered that many of their patrons were more than willing to plunk one, two and three dollars into a machine—if they were reasonably assured of frequent payouts and hopeful of hitting greater jackpots. Now, patrons could choose between three-, four-, and five-reel machines, and finally, in 1980, Bally introduced its series E machines, the first computer-controlled microprocessor slots, making possible giant, linked-progressive jackpots which became the staple of Bally's newest and fiercest competitor, I.G.T.

Bally's machines were slick and fascinating. With the introduction of the microprocessor, astute prophets of casino profits could see the handwriting on the wall. The slots were about to inherit the reel earth just as computers were inheriting the real earth!

Today, many manufacturers vie for the still-rapidly-growing casino slot trade with Bally and I.G.T. (International Game Technology) the leaders in the field. In gaming, as in most areas of economic life, with competition usually comes a better deal for the astute consumer—in this case, the players. Of course, to get the best bang for your hard-earned buck, a knowledge of how the machines work is the starting point for an attempt at breaking the one-armed bandits.

3

Mechanical Evolution

Where Did Those Incredibly "Smart" Machines Come From?

Evolution is an interesting study. It informs us that humanity's most ancient ancestor was shared in common with today's chimpanzees and gorillas. Our two contemporary simian cousins share the same evolutionary branch of the same evolutionary tree as do we. Yet it is only we humans who can appreciate the rhyming of "tree" and "we" at the conclusion of the previous sentence. Indeed, it is only we humans who have constructed a massive planet-wide (albeit shaky) civilization, developed extensive oral and written languages, created religion and science and technology, explored beyond our planet and—most important of all—built casinos.

Although I credit gorillas and chimps with great intelligence compared to other life forms (after all, they *are* our cousins!), I just wouldn't feel comfortable going to one for a medical diagnosis or finding one in the cockpit of the jet on my next flight to Las Vegas. They're just not the same as us.

Of course, an alien from another galaxy might confuse the three species—man, gorilla, and chimp—due to superficial resemblances. We are all humanoids after all. And we do function biologically about the same. But when it comes to "mind" or "brain" or "insight" or "creativity," we are worlds apart. Here our shared looks are deceiving. The inner consciousness of man surpasses that of our cousins despite the similarity of form. True, some humans are probably dumber than some gorillas and chimps—truthfully, I'm convinced that some humans are dumber than inanimate objects, which at least know how to remain quiet and unobtrusive and non-violent. But overall, humans, despite sharing the same basic shape as our cousins, are the upscale end of our evolutionary family.

Today's slot machines are the upscale end of a mechanical evolution every bit as dramatic as the one that produced us. And although today's machines share superficial resemblances with the slots of the past, they are as unlike them as Einstein was unlike an ape. The interior workings of contemporary slots are a far cry from the clanging, banging, gear-driven slots of the past. Today's machines are "smart," and to have a possibility of beating them, you have to be smart too. You have to understand them and you have to (metaphorically) *outwit* them!

Know this: The slot machine is your enemy. Your goal is to beat it so badly that it pours out its lifeblood, i.e. its coins, in a stream so large that attendants have to come running to help stanch the flow. But to beat your enemy, you have to know your enemy. You have to know where he came from and where he is now. You have to know how he thinks.

Don't think I'm being facetious when I say that today's slot machines are "smart." The machines *are* smart. They have smart creators and programmers. They have smart casino executives positioning them in the casinos in such a way as to maximize the casinos' profits and the players' losses. The new slot machines are almost tamperproof and it takes a computer genius (or a guy with a sledgehammer) to get one to malfunction. The new machines regulate themselves in almost every way. They know and keep track of their payouts; they generally know when they are being tampered with; they even know when they aren't functioning up to par! They can follow the play of slot-club members; how much so-and-so has won or lost over a given period of time. The new machines have pleasing personalities and they wear colorful clothing. Despite all this, the new machines are still bandits, a trait they share in common with their more ancient cousins.

The Early Models

The early slot machines were *mechanical* devices whose internal landscape featured gears, levers and pulleys. They were "dumb" machines, easily beaten by astute cheats and sometimes by skilled "handle pumpers" or "arm twisters." These were the machines that were first to be dubbed "one-armed bandits." Indeed, they earned that name for two reasons. The first was simply functional. The arm was an intricate part of the slot machine process. You put in your coin and you pulled the arm. Pulling it turned the gears which in turn spun the reels. The arm was therefore the direct cause of the resulting symbols which appeared—and therefore a direct cause of you usually losing your money. Even though smart tacticians could beat these dumb machines, more often than not, the players were even dumber than the machines they played, often having no idea of what devastating percentages they faced—hence the appellation, correctly applied, of "one-armed bandits."

The original slot machine, the Liberty Bell, had three reels with 10 symbols on each reel strip. Each strip rotated independently and stopped in a left to right, one, two, three order. If the machine were played according to design, then whatever symbol appeared was the result of a random process—the spinning of the reels. Each stop was as likely as any other stop to be selected.

These early slot machines were designed to hold between 10 and 50 cents of every dollar played. Of course, being mere mechanical devices, the Liberty Bell was easily tampered with, not only by cheating players, but by some of the unscrupulous vendors who leased them. It was not unusual for machines to be "gaffed," thus preventing the reels from coming to rest on certain combinations.

On the 10-spot, three-reel machines, there were 1,000 possible combinations that could occur. The jackpot, lining up three bells (assuming one bell per strip), was a 999 to one shot. That's because $10/1 \times 10/1 \times 10/1 = 1000/1$, giving you one possible win out of 1,000 possible combinations. Thus your odds of winning would be 999 to one (if the machine weren't rigged!).

Of course, the machine did not pay off at true value for every possible combination—there's no profit in that. Most combinations didn't pay anything and most of the ones that did pay, didn't pay off at true odds. Naturally, a slot machine was designed to give back less than it took in—otherwise who would want to own or lease one for his establishment? Thus it was a one-armed bandit if you were a player and a one-armed gold mine if you were an owner or vendor.

It still is.

Here's how a "typical" bell machine at the beginning of the twentieth century figured its payback percentage based upon the number of reels, the symbols on each, and their payouts.

Symbol	Reel 1	Reel 2	Reel 3
Bell	one	one	one
Hearts	one	one	two
Diamonds	one	one	three
Spades	two	two	two
Clubs	five	five	(blank)
Symbol	(blank)	(blank)	two

Combination	Coins Paid	×	Reels: $1 \times 2 \times 3$	=	Total Coins Paid
two clubs	2	×	$5 \times 5 \times 8$	=	400 coins
two clubs & symbol	4	×	$5 \times 5 \times 2$	=	200 coins
three spades	8	×	$2 \times 2 \times 2$	=	64 coins
three diamonds	12	×	$1 \times 1 \times 3$	=	36 coins
three hearts	14	×	$1 \times 1 \times 2$	=	28 coins
three bells	22	×	$1 \times 1 \times 1$	=	22 coins
			total coins paid	=	750 coins

Out of 1,000 possible outcomes and one thousand coins put through the machine ($10 \times 10 \times 10$), 750 coins are paid back, making this machine retain 25 cents of every dollar played for a payback percentage of 75 percent.

The Middle Models

The mechanical slots had their day from the 1890s to the early 1950s, only to be surpassed by a superior model, the electromechanical machines, which dominated casino play from the late 1950s until the mid-1970s. These beauties were a giant leap up the evolutionary machine ladder as they could accommodate multiple-coin play, multiple-pay lines, larger jackpots, as well as progressive jackpots and "buy-a-pay" lines. They were also somewhat more difficult to tamper with and cheaters had to work overtime to outwit them. You could not "finesse" the arm of these new machines and expect to win because once the arm was pulled it merely alerted the circuitry to start the reels rolling. The arm was now only the sparkplug, so to speak, and it was not the direct cause of the reels' rotation. If you wanted to cheat, you had to get "inside" the machine in some way—and clever cheaters discovered those ways in abundance.

However, as sophisticated as these machines were, they were not "bright" and had to be constantly supervised by casino employees lest they trip up and start malfunctioning. Their flashing lights, musical sounds, coin-holding proper-ties, and potentially giant jackpots were impressive and ac-counted, in part, for the explosive growth of slot play in the late 1960s and early 1970s. Their superficial outer design be-came the norm and pattern for all subsequent slot machines: a window display with multiple pay and play features, an arm, perhaps a button, to stimulate the circuitry, a large hop-per and tray for coin payouts, and a pleasing and colorful look and disposition that bordered on the musical.

Unlike the 10-stop, three-reel, mechanical one-armed bandits, the electromechanical banditos had anywhere from three to five reels with 20 or more stops on each, making pos-sible a wider variety of hits and payouts—and much longer odds on some of the larger jackpots. Still, the machines oper-ated in precisely the same fashion as their more primitive forebears, only instead of gears and levers, electricity was the dynamic force. Yet the reels still operated independently and it was still their spinning and eventual stopping that deter-mined the outcome for the player. With the increased reel space and the increased number of reels, the probabilities were staggering, as the following chart will indicate.

# of Reels	Stops	# of Possible Combinations
three	10	1,000
three	20	8,000
three	22	10,648
three	25	15,625
three	32	32,768
three	45	91,125
three	64	262,144
three	84	592,704
four	20	160,000
four	22	234,256
four	25	390,625
four	63	15,752,961
four	64	16,777,216
five	22	5,153,632

Today, the electromechanicals can still be found in many casinos but you will not see them reproducing themselves for they are now an evolutionary dead end thanks to the new "sapien-slots." In biological evolution, the age of the dinosaurs lasted approximately 150 million years. Then the mammals took over. Now, for at least 10,000 years, man has reigned supreme on this planet—subjugating and annihilating the lesser orders. We are *homo sapiens sapiens*, the thinking creatures, the rulers of the mammals. In the world of gambling, the table games are the dinosaurs, and the early mechanical and the electromechanical slots are the non-sapiens mammals. And now their betters are displacing them at a frightening rate.

Those Smart Machines

They look just the way a slot machine should look, for they are made in the image and likeness of their ancestors. They have arms; they have reels; they have bells and lights and hoppers. You put a coin or coins in, pull the arm or press the button; the reels spin and stop: one, two, three and, maybe, four, five, six. And then you know if you've won or lost and you begin the process all over again.

But these new machines are to the traditional slots what today's gourmet-dining humans are to gorillas rooting under logs for some succulent grubs and bugs. There's a world of difference; a world of difference that exists not in form or physique, which are similar, but in the cranial areas, in that inner consciousness which is the heart and soul of a being or a slot machine!

The new computer-driven slots are smart. They are the height of slot-machine evolution, for built into each one is a complicated design program consisting of a number of microchips that function as the brain or "consciousness" of the mechanism. These new slots are not run by gears and levers or electromechanical circuits, but by the microprocessor units (computer chips and integrated circuitry) that generate a continuous series of random numbers, which will, when properly interpreted by the computer's "brain," correspond to the various symbols and sequences on the various reels.

The microchips will determine the order and frequency of every symbol's appearance; how much is to be paid by the machine; what payouts require the intervention of a human; which lights will flash during the payout; what sounds will be heard. The consciousness of the machine knows if its parts are in good working order and are functioning perfectly. The machine knows when it is being tampered with and will quickly take steps to protect its precious treasure—those coins. These new machines are loyal to their makers and their casino masters, because they will shut themselves down—literally die— to stop would-be looters from having their way.

Keep in mind that the symbols, or rather the random numbers that will correspond to a symbol sequence, are constantly being selected—*even when the machine isn't being played!* That's correct. Pass of bank of seemingly quiescent slot machines and in reality there is feverish activity going on behind their placid facades. Every fraction of a second, the random number generator is selecting a random number between zero to upwards of five billion (so ponder the odds on those giant megajackpots). This process will go on undisturbed until the machine dies, that is, until it is unplugged or shut off or some disgruntled slot player hits it with a sledgehammer.

And those machines are sitting there. Busy, busy. Yet they are waiting. For you, the player, to join them in the frenetic activities.

They are waiting for a player to initiate a public display of the single probability that has been selected at that precise moment by the mind or ghost in the machine.

Wait a minute, you might say, doesn't the slot machine need a person to pull the arm or push the button to activate the reels which in turn spin randomly and stop wherever they will? Isn't that the way it was done in the past? Didn't the reels spin and land randomly in the past and that's how a sequence was determined? Isn't that how it's still done?

The past is dead.

That is not the way the new slots work. Those reels spin to give the slot player a show and to make him or her feel comfortable because real (reel) change is unsettling to humans. Slot players want to think they are playing machines with which they are familiar. Remember the movie *The Invasion of the Body Snatchers*, where giant seed pods from outer space came down and duplicated the bodies of humans? Remember how the humans were the same in every way, down to the last scar, but friends and relatives could "sense" a difference? Well, the new slot machines look exactly like the old ones but they are *not* the same.

The reels are essentially irrelevant appendages that merely inform the player of what sequence of symbols the microchip has PRESELECTED. You could conceivably do away with the reels altogether and simply let the machine digest your money and spit out coins when its brain tells it to. You don't even need all the fancy lights and bells and symbols. You could have a blank machine face with an opening to take coins and an opening to spew coins. The inner awareness of the machine is determining everything—albeit, it is determining everything at random. Thus, we are dealing with *random determinism!*

So when you hear someone say: "I just left that machine and that jerk sits down a few seconds later, puts in two quarters and bingo! he hits for a million. He took my jackpot," you no longer have to believe him or be concerned about how the gods treat us like sport. The sequence ordering that jackpot was there for a millisecond. Even if the someone who just complained had been at the machine, the very next play was not the jackpot. Between the time Player One got up and Player Two sat down, say five seconds, hundreds, if not thousands, of different probabilities had already been played out in the private consciousness of the machine. The winning of the big jackpot is a synchronistic event—the cojoining of coins in and random number selected and player informed. In other words, it's luck!

To help you understand the reality of what you face, picture this. As you put your coins in the machine (one . . . two . . . three) many sequences have come and gone in the mind of the machine. Now . . . you . . . push . . . the . . . button. Even during the split second before the wheels spin, sequences are flashing in and out of the microchip brain, until a sequence is selected that then determines what will appear on the first, second, third and, perhaps, fourth and fifth reels. Had you paused a nanosecond to wipe your brow as you placed coins in the machine, a totally different sequence would have appeared on the reels. Your playing merely reveals the will of the machine, nothing more. Metaphorically, when it comes to today's slots, trees are falling constantly in the forest with no one there to hear them—but as soon as the coins connect with the machine, you will be allowed to find out which tree just happened to fall at that moment outside your earshot.

Here's another thing to ponder. On today's smart machines, it is essentially irrelevant how many symbols there are on a given reel because the total number of symbols has nothing whatsoever to do with how often they will appear. The microchip randomly determines what will occur.

For argument's sake, let us say that we take that old bell machine from the turn of the century and give it a brain transplant. We take out the primitive and cumbersome inner workings and substitute our brave new microprocessor. In our old scenario, there were 1,000 possible outcomes whose probability was determined by the number of symbols on each reel. Since every reel had one bell, there was a one in 10 chance of a given reel coming up bell. Thus, the odds were nine to one on a single reel. As stated previously, the three bells appearing together were 999 to one.

But now we have a smart machine, and watch what it can do. Say we don't want to have the bells only come up once every thousand spins. We want them to come up on average once *every other* spin, but without having to go through the bother of putting more of them on the actual reels. The microprocessor simply does the following: It selects bells on each reel eight out of every 10 spins. Then we have $8 \times 8 \times 8 = 512$ three-bell hits out of 1,000 spins. It is irrelevant how many bells are actually on the reel because the reel merely shows us the will of the machine.

This type of programming, in a somewhat more complicated way, is exactly what the new machines do. Even though the reels may contain 20 or 22 "stops," the microprocessor can act as if each reel has hundreds of stops because it is deciding what symbols will appear and when, not the reels themselves. You could theoretically have 20 bars on one 22-stop reel in a machine that is programmed never to select a bar on that particular reel! Those bars will flash by but it will always be a lemon that will appear on the pay line.

If a given machine is programmed to pay back 90 percent of the money put in it, in the long run that machine will pay back approximately 90 percent. If the machine is programmed not to give out a giant jackpot until a given number of coins have been played, then there are no jackpots until those coins are played. If a machine is programmed not to return a cent, then no one wins on that machine, and it doesn't matter how many bars and stars and logos flash past your eyes—everything will come up lemons!

Of course, two things prevent casinos from programming all their machines to pay nothing. The first is simply that no one would play these no-return machines and the casinos wouldn't have any giant pictures of smiling winners to hang on their walls in order to encourage more people to play. It's one thing to buck slightly more or less unfavorable odds or probabilities, it's another to buck a singular, negative certainty.

The second reason that casinos won't program all their machines to pay back nothing is because they aren't allowed to. Most states have some laws that the casinos must follow concerning the general programming of their slots. These laws were made for the benefit of the players. For example, in New Jersey a casino cannot program a machine to return less than 83 percent of the money put in it. In Nevada, the laws are a little looser (so, on average, are the machines) and it is theoretically possible for two models of the exact same machine sitting side by side to be paying 98 and 80 percent respectively. In a real sense, related machines have different personalities—some are generous, some are stingy—even if they come from the same family!

The Machine Families

Walk through the casinos of America and you will notice hundreds of seemingly different machines all with their own individual names such as *Neptune's Treasure, the Fabulous Fifties, Black Gold, Lucky 7's, Stars and Bars* and on and on. In reality, most of today's slot machines belong to three distinct families of machines: "multipliers," "multiple-line-pay" machines and "buy-your-pay" machines.

If two differently named machines require maximum coin for the big jackpot, or if they reward you with a better percentage payout for other wins when you put in maximum coins, and if all wins line up on the center line, chances are that no matter what individual name a machine carries such as *Harry's Crazy Eights* or *Lenny's Looney Nines*, they are exactly the same kind of machine. They may have different packaging, different symbols on their display reels, and make different noises when they go off, but essentially they are multipliers—that is, machines that reward multiple-coin play with better payouts.

On the other hand, if they are machines that reward play on more than one line, that is, one coin pays on line one, two coins pay on line two, three coins pay on line three and so forth, then these are "multiple-line" machines. No matter their individual names, they come from the "multiple-line-pay" family. When you play these machines, the line will light up as the coins are inserted. (And *always* wait for the lines to light up to make sure the machine has recorded your intended play.)

The third family of machines has a somewhat checkered reputation and can be considered the black sheep of the slot machine kingdom. These are the "buy-your-pay" machines and they can be killers.

Although this is a single-line payout machine it does not reward all hits unless the maximum number of coins are played. Unlike the multiplier, which rewards all hits but gives a better percentage win based on maximum coin play, the "buy-your-pay" machines will make distinctions. Thus, the first coin will allow a win, say, on cherries appearing. But if apricots appear, you lose if you are playing only one coin. However, put a second coin in and then you can win on both apricots and cherries. But a watermelon's appearance will leave you dry. Put that third coin in and cherries, apricots *and* watermelons are all on your winning menu.

These machines have caused countless players frustration and agony when they see the big jackpot sequence hit only to be informed that they haven't won anything since they hadn't played maximum coin. In fact, one of the famous tales concerning one of these machines has a husband belting out his wife who, while he was in the bathroom, decided to save him money by playing only one coin. She hit the jackpot sequence—a $50,000 win!—but didn't have enough coins in, so she won nothing. Her husband, discovering he had hit it big only to lose it, hit his wife a big one right in the chops, knocking her unconscious. This supposedly happened at the Golden Nugget in downtown Las Vegas.

I spoke to one woman in Las Vegas who lost the jackpot that way—twice!

"The first time, I had been playing for about an hour, just one coin at a time," she said, "and then I hit the big one, three bars. Only nothing happened. Playing one coin I realized I wouldn't get the super jackpot but I figured I'd get something. Nothing. The second time was a carbon copy of the first, only this time it was three 7's that I hit. Again I received nothing. I always thought that maximum coin gave the best payback but I thought you got some kind of payback if you hit with less."

Had the machine been a "multiplier," the lady would have received whatever the maximum win was for the number of coins played had she hit the jackpot sequence. If it had been a "multiple-line" machine, the appropriate line would have lit up and shown her what her possibilities were. Unfortunately, the "buy-your-pay" machines make you "buy" your right to go for the jackpot sequence even though the pay-out is usually on the center line for all coins. Thus, if you don't read the directions on the machine carefully, you can find yourself hitting a "big one" and getting a big nothing.

It goes without saying that an astute slots player will always know what type of machine he or she is playing before putting in any money. It's tough enough to win when you play perfectly but mistakes can cost you dearly.

The Question of Casino Cheating

One question remains, however. If these machines are so smart, could they be programmed to cheat the customers? Every casino executive I spoke to for this book stated emphatically that while the machines probably could be programmed to "cheat," it would be silly, if not downright idiotic, for casinos to allow it.

Stated one Las Vegas slot manager: "We have hundreds of machines that are bringing in exactly the revenues we want from them. Why cheat? Why risk losing your license? Why risk going to jail? We are making our profits; it would be the height of foolishness to cheat customers. Also, with the tight controls and the constant examination of both the machines' actual performance and their theoretical programming, it would be next to impossible to cheat."

However, one computer expert I spoke to had a different slant. Dr. James Schneider (not his real name) has worked for both NASA and Grumman designing computer programs for military and civilian aircraft, as well as for the space program. He has also been a consultant to various "smart" machine manufacturers in the United States and abroad.

He said: "First, you have to define what you mean by cheating in the context of a game where the house has an edge. In Las Vegas, you can program machines to withhold however much you want, so short of having a machine that has an arm that reaches out and takes money from the pockets of unwary patrons passing by, there would be no need to cheat—just program the machine to take whatever percentage you wanted.

"However, let's get more sophisticated in our definition of 'cheating.' Say you wanted to design a program that used psychological principles to increase the total amount played at your machines. You could easily design a program that encouraged individuals to play more. For example, let us say that you need maximum coin to win a jackpot. Now, a player puts in less than the maximum and all of a sudden he gets the winner. Only he doesn't win anything because he didn't put in the required number of coins [see our ladies above]. From this point on, you have a good chance that he'll always play maximum coin.

"You could have a sub-program that reads the playing of less-than-maximum coin as an invitation to hit the jackpots more often than the overt programming indicates. Let us say that it's ten thousand to one to hit a particular jackpot. But your sub-program reduces that to a 100 to one for less than maximum coin, just to let people see that [jackpot] sequence appear. It doesn't cost the casino anything and it's a great incentive. Now, when you study the spread sheets closely, you don't want to see the jackpot sequence appearing so often, so a part of the sub-programming is a camouflage program that covers up what actually appeared. Technically, this might not even be cheating since you could substitute the 'losing' jackpot sequence for any other losing sequence. The player wasn't going to win anyway since he hadn't put in the correct number of coins and instead of three oranges appearing [a losing sequence] or whatever, the jackpot sequence is substituted. But a check of the regular programming and the algorithms and performance of the machine would show those three oranges as having appeared. That, in a nutshell, is a simplistic way of showing how easily these machines can be made to do what you want them to."

What about cheating in venues that require a minimum payback on all machines? Could you "rig" a machine to pay back far less but appear to be paying back more?

Schneider states: "Absolutely. Remember that probability is a long range, statistical study. Just because a machine is supposedly programmed to return a given percentage doesn't mean it actually will. Check a machine that has been operating for a day or a week or even longer and you will see that it can deviate quite a bit from its programming—in fact, deviation is a requirement of proper random programming. So a casino could cheat by putting in machines that deviate like crazy on the first ten thousand pulls or the fifth ten thousand pulls or whatever. In those selected ten thousand pulls, more losing sequences are programmed to come up. When the sequence is over, the machine returns to randomness for the next hundred-thousand pulls before becoming non-random again. Of course, again you would have to put in a subprogram that covers up for the cheating. Or, just as easily, you could declare the machine's programming or execution of the programming defective and reprogram it. That would show good faith and, of course, the individuals who were 'cheated' would never know and would get nothing back."

But did Dr. Schneider really think casinos would do such a thing?

"Who knows? In America, I doubt it, but in other countries with less regulation, I guess it's a possibility. Slot machine manufacturers program based on the desires of the buyer. If the buyer wants something, as long as it's not illegal to actually program a machine a certain way or, at least, not get caught at it, then I guess it's always a possibility."

So when it comes to slots, it's not "let the buyer beware," it's "let the players be wary!"

4

S-T-R-E-T-C-H-I-N-G

... That Devastating House Edge

It's no secret how the casinos of America make their money. Almost all games have been structured to give the house a mathematical edge on almost every bet. I say "almost every bet" because there are some bets where the house doesn't have the mathematical edge—the odds bet in craps, for example, is a fair bet that theoretically in the long run will be a break-even proposition for both the house and the player. In blackjack, certain games can be theoretically beaten in the long run by skillful card counters, who hold a long-term edge over the casino. You also have a theoretical chance to beat real poker players, certain video-poker games, and pai-gow poker in the long run.

Sadly, there is no theoretical way to beat a slot machine that has been programmed properly to take a certain percentage of the total play. Short of taking a hammer and breaking one open, or using other illegal means, the slot player faces a theoretically long-term losing proposition.

Of course, the fact that a theoretical edge can be gotten by players at certain games is not sufficient to state that categorically everyone who plays those games will win. The reverse is also true. Just because the casino has a theoretical edge over the player on a given game does not mean that the player *must* lose. For example, blackjack has always had a reputation for being beatable, yet very few players have ever beaten the game in the long run, as the casino ledgers clearly indicate. Most players are underfinanced and unskilled. Blackjack profits are staggering for the casinos. The level of skill required to beat blackjack is great. You must know how to recognize beatable games, have the proper strategies to play these games, the proper mental discipline and money-management techniques and, with all these, be a skilled enough actor or actress not to let the casinos know just how skilled you really are since you don't want to be asked to leave.

And you need luck.

I have never been one to discount the idea of luck—even in games where I have a slight mathematical edge. Again, if we look at blackjack, we can see how luck plays a part. At best, a skilled card counter can get a one to two percent edge over the house in the long run. Truthfully, I think it's closer to one percent than two percent. That's a small edge and just a few playing mistakes, mental lapses or poor money management moves can easily wipe out that edge on a given night or a given year.

A friend of mine, Alan Tinker, who was recently inducted into the Blackjack Hall of Fame, and is as good a blackjack player as anyone, has been on an 18-month losing streak as I write this! During this time, I played at the same tables with him on a number of occasions—he played flawlessly. I won. He lost. Why? I got the cards. He didn't. I had good luck. He had bad luck. So what has Alan done about it? "I'm reducing the size of my bets. Until my luck turns around, I'm starting off with much lower bets than usual. I don't want to lose so much during this cold streak that I won't be able to recoup when my luck turns around."

Keeping losses as low as possible in losing streaks allows a player to be within shooting distance of a win if and when his luck turns around. Truly savvy gamblers know this is the only way to have a chance at winning in the long run. You cannot allow yourself to fall into so deep a hole that no amount of landfill will get you out.

I spoke to the Captain about this. I wanted to see if he had any ideas on how to tackle slot playing with its built-in disadvantage. As many of my readers know, the Captain is the greatest craps player in history and has developed wonderful playing strategies to tackle and beat this mathematically negative game. (See my books *Beat the Craps out of the Casinos: How to Play Craps and Win!* and *Guerrilla Gambling: How to Beat the Casinos at Their Own Games!*)

States the Captain: "The whole key to playing any game with some chance for long-term success—whether it be a negative-expectancy game like craps, or a positive-expectancy game like blackjack, is the player's ability to stretch his money over time. If you have a thousand dollars, you don't want to lose nine hundred of it in the first hour of play—especially if you intend to play for the next several days. The longer you can stay at a game, and the more you can stretch your money, the better chance you have of hitting a hot streak or, in the case of slots, getting a big jackpot. But you have to stretch the money you have designated for gambling—not lose that money and dig in for more money that wasn't earmarked for gambling purposes. There's a difference between *stretching* money and *losing* money. In the former you are positioning yourself to take advantage of good luck, in the latter you are positioning yourself to have bad luck take advantage of you. If I were given a choice of losing a thousand dollars over 10 days or of losing a thousand dollars in one day, I'd rather spread it over the 10 days."

The Captain continued: "I realize that the slots are a tougher proposition than craps because there are no human factors involved. Part of my success at craps has been my ability to avoid horrendous rolls and to select rhythmic rollers. I also know when to get off my numbers. You don't really have those variables when you are playing the slots. The edge is built into the programming of the individual machine. So to stretch your money at slots, you have to find the best possible machines to play; machines that give you the greatest return for your money so that you can last longer—and maybe get that jackpot."

To be an effective slots player, then, requires its own set of skills.

> 1. You have to know which casinos give their slot players the best return.

> 2. You have to know which machines will return the best percentage in those casinos.

> 3. You have to have some method for locating these machines within a casino.

> 4. You have to develop clear playing and money-management strategies for tackling the machines you've selected to play.

I'll cover each of these in upcoming chapters.

However, in this chapter let us address the Captain's idea that the key to having a chance to win is the ability to s-t-r-e-t-c-h your money over time. There's no secret concerning how to do that in slots—play machines that give the best return. You'll be able to play longer on these machines and have the best chance for a win.

Casinos know this too. That's why in casino advertising you constantly see such phrases as: "Our Slot Machines Are the Loosest!" "Best Slots in Town!" "98% Return!" Casino publicity departments realize that most slot players have a vague notion that playing "loose" machines is better than playing "tight" ones and that the definitions of "loose" and "tight" have something to do with the average return the machine gives out. Naturally, if you were to play a "loose" machine until infinity, the result would be the same as if you had played a "tight" one—you'd go broke.

Not being immortal, no slot player will be playing so long. Still, the casinos know another thing that's money in the bank for them—they know that most slot players are not content to put their money through the machine once; that the hundred or thousand dollars that you brought will be subjected over and over to the grinding effect of their house edge, and that most slot players will lose every last coin before they stop playing. That's because they play their money through the machine over and over.

The following chart will show you the effects of different returns on the bankroll of a player who starts with $100. From a high return of 99 percent to a low of 83 percent, let us see the grinding effects of the house edge on your money. Also note how many pulls of the handle you have for each percentage and remember this: the more pulls of the handle you have for the same investment means the better chance you have of hitting a jackpot! Keep in mind that the player is putting through that same $100. Thus, he plays it through the first time and gets back $99 on the 99 percent machine. Then he plays that $99 through and receives $98.01 because 99 percent of $99 is $98.01. Then he plays the $98.01 through and gets back 99 percent of that. As you will see, in slots, unlike life, the race is to the s-l-o-w-e-s-t!

Plays	99% Return	93% Return	88% Return	83% Return
0	$100	$100	$100	$100
1	$99	$93	$88	$83
2	$98.01	$86.49	$77.44	$68.89
3	$97.03	$80.44	$68.15	$57.18
4	$96.06	$74.81	$59.97	$47.46
5	$95.10	$69.57	$52.77	$39.39
6	$94.15	$64.70	$46.43	$32.69
7	$93.21	$60.73	$40.86	$27.13
8	$92.27	$55.96	$35.96	$22.52
9	$91.35	$52.04	$31.64	$18.69
10	$90.44	$48.40	$27.84	$15.51
11	$89.53	$45.01	$24.50	$12.87
12	$88.64	$41.86	$21.56	$10.68
13	$87.75	$38.93	$18.97	$ 9.40
14	$86.87	$36.20	$16.69	$ 7.80
15	$86.00	$33.67	$14.69	$ 6.47
16	$85.15	$31.31	$12.93	$ 5.37
17	$84.29	$29.12	$11.38	$ 4.46
18	$83.45	$27.08	$10.01	$ 3.70
19	$82.62	$25.19	$ 8.81	$ 3.07
20	$81.79	$23.42	$ 7.75	$ 2.55
21	$80.97	$21.78	$ 6.82	$ 2.12
22	$80.16	$20.26	$ 6.00	$ 1.76
23	$79.36	$18.84	$ 5.28	$ 1.46
24	$78.57	$17.52	$ 4.65	$ 1.21
25	$77.78	$16.30	$ 4.09	$ 1.00

26	$77.00	$15.16	$ 3.60	$ .83
27	$76.23	$14.09	$ 3.17	$ .69
28	$75.47	$13.11	$ 2.79	$ .57
29	$74.71	$12.19	$ 2.46	$ .47
30	$73.97	$11.34	$ 2.16	$ .39
31	$73.23	$10.54	$ 1.90	$ .32
32	$72.50	$ 9.81	$ 1.67	$ .27
33	$71.77	$ 9.12	$ 1.47	$ .22
34	$71.06	$ 8.48	$ 1.29	$ .18
35	$70.34	$ 7.88	$ 1.14	$ .15
36	$69.64	$ 7.33	$ 1.00	$ .12
37	$68.94	$ 6.82	$ .88	$ .10
38	$68.26	$ 6.34	$ .77	$ .08
39	$67.57	$ 5.90	$ .68	$ .07
40	$66.90	$ 5.49	$ .60	$ .06

Okay, as you can see, the player playing at the 99-percent-return machine has slightly more than two-thirds of his bankroll left after theoretically playing his money through the machine 40 times, while the 93-percent-return player has approximately five percent left and the 88 percent-return player has sixth-tenths of one percent remaining. Our lowly 83-percent-return player has six-hundreths of one percent of his initial bankroll left after putting his money through the machine 40 times! If you were going to bet on who had a better chance to come home a winner or come home with any money at all—who would you choose?

The above chart is a graphically brutal display of just how devastating a few percentage points can be when you play the slots. It also clearly demonstrates that to have any chance at all of coming home a winner you must s-t-r-e-t-c-h your money over time and hope to hit some jackpots along the way.

In Atlantic City, where 83 percent is the minimum theoretical return allowed, you can find machines that are returning 95 and 96 percent. In Las Vegas, you can actually find machines paying 99 percent—but, with no lower limit, you can also find machines paying back 75 percent or less.

You've got to know what to look for!

5

All Machines Are
Not Created Equal!

In the last chapter we saw the varying yet universally devastating effects of the house edge on a starting bankroll of $100. Even at a 99-percent machine, you were down one-third of your bankroll after 40 plays through your bankroll. The question naturally arises: Why would anyone play the machines knowing this? Perhaps you shouldn't. Purists would argue that any negative expectation game is essentially a waste of time, effort and, more importantly, money.

Well, I'm not a purist.

The play-through-bankroll runs of the last chapter, you could reasonably argue, are just theoretical constructs based on the long-run expectations contained in probability theory and do not necessarily hold for short-term play. This is not a foolish argument since very few short runs reflect probability theory perfectly. There are always deviations from the norm, such as streaks of given numbers in roulette or craps appearing, or not appearing, as the case may be. Indeed, I have a friend who made quite a bit of money in high school by betting other kids that on 36 rolls of the dice the seven would *not* come up exactly its theoretically probable six times. So, the fact that the house can have a rather monstrous edge on a given machine does not mean that a person must *automatically* lose. In the short run of any game, regardless of whether it's a player-positive or a player-negative expectation game, anything can and does happen. Unless something is a one-hundred-percent certainty, the short run results can look as unlike probability theory projections as a horse looks like a house.

Still, the greater the house edge, the greater the *probability* of losing your horse *over time*. Time is the great nemesis of man and while it might heal all wounds, it only does so to bring you ever closer to your inevitable death. Yes, and time is the great enemy of most gamblers as it takes its toll on their bankrolls by wearing away at them. Like a single drop of water hitting a stone, eventually time will cause even the biggest bankrolls to be worn full of holes. It is not an arcane secret that to have any chance of winning, you must make the best use of your gambling dollars. To do this, you have to seek out machines that give you the best bang for your buck by wearing away at your bankroll the least over time.

Purists might not agree with this, but people gamble for different reasons and, with the possible exception of an uncontrollable compulsion that sinks both self and others in a swamp of debt, degradation and humiliation, whatever the reasons for an individual's gambling, they are all equally valid. If the theoretical shot at big money is a sufficient lure and thrill to warrant a person's bucking negative odds and playing the slots, then fine. You decide why you gamble—for fun, for profit, for adrenaline rushes and thrills; for a hobby, for cordial associations with other gamblers or for lack of something better to do with your spare time. Whatever your reason, that is sufficient reason to do it and it is sufficient reason to do it wisely.

Still, when all the reasons for risking hard-earned money are listed, it is always more thrilling to win!

I think that if you can keep the house edge under two percent and figure in the comps the casinos give you for your play, then you have a reasonable chance of winning—in short-run and, perhaps, even long-run play. That's because your money buys you more pulls of the handle or presses of the button on machines that are paying back in the vicinity of 98 percent. A little luck and a few comps against a two percent edge is all you need to win, whereas you need a lot of luck against a 12 percent edge and there's no number of comps that can make up for that.

The problem facing you as a slot player is simply stated— how do you find machines that return 98 percent? Even if these machines are in a casino, comfortably nestled between machines paying back 83 and 88 percent, how do you find them? It's not as if most casinos put signs on the machines telling their customers that here indeed is a "good payer!" Yet some casinos actually do this. Bally's in Las Vegas has advertised carousels of certain machines with the promo that these machines are returning approximately 98 percent of all money played. Not bad—if it's really true.

For argument's sake, let us say that you can find machines that return 98 percent. Can you have any confidence that long-term play might, just *might,* yield long-term profits? Yes and no. If we put aside a huge dose of luck, say winning a jackpot so big that no amount of future slot-machine gambling can diminish it, then the answer to whether you have a possibility of winning a profit all depends on your definition of profit. If you get various casino comps for your play (free or discounted rooms, free meals, special promotions that increase certain wins during certain times) and these, averaged with your theoretical long-run losses from the slots, equal a profit, then in my estimation you're a candidate for being a long-term winner.

I happen to consider casino comps to be money in my pocket. What is the cost of a room? Fifty dollars? A hundred and fifty dollars? Well, that 50 or 150 dollars should be factored in. That free meal has a monetary value—what is it? If you don't factor in comps, even on machines that offer 98 percent returns, it would be difficult, though not impossible, to play for the long run and come out a winner—unless you get quite lucky and hit a monster jackpot, always a hoped-for possibility.

Regardless of how you personally feel about comps and their value to you, the fact remains that you should seek out the best possible machines to play. That's common sense. Yet often finding good machines is easier said than done. Even carousels that are advertised as having a 98 percent return are sometimes misleading. Is the return an average that includes a progressive jackpot that skews the results? A carousel might average 98 percent as a whole because the jackpot going to one individual is large enough to make a bunch of machines that are actually paying back 95 percent (or 92 percent or whatever) appear to be averaging 98 percent. Here's an instructive quote concerning the slots from a casino manager in Las Vegas that I'm lifting verbatim from my own book, *Guerrilla Gambling: How to Beat the Casinos at Their Own Games!*

"The players have to beware when a casino advertises that it pays back a large percentage on its slots. You have to find out if the slots being referred to are progressives with a big jackpot and whether that jackpot's theoretical hitting is calculated into the win percentages. If it is, a machine that is advertised as returning 97 percent may actually be returning much less because the jackpot is figured into the return. Sure, on average, because of the huge jackpot, the machines in this grouping are returning 97 percent, but the jackpot is skewing the figures. In reality, people are losing a lot more and only one person at a time and over an extended period of time will hit the jackpot. Before that jackpot is hit, we can still advertise that the payout is 97 percent. However, every day we'll be taking much, much more and getting interest on it so that when we pay out the jackpot, we're not even losing the total jackpot monies. Of course, we'll put the winner's picture on the wall and that will encourage even more people to put money in those particular machines."

Despite the mystery that has traditionally surrounded the slot machine payouts and programming, certain "truths" have been generally agreed upon by slot authorities based upon the casinos' own slot statistics and the informed guesswork of the aforementioned authorities. Luckily, some states have mandatory reporting regulations so we can be fairly certain of the viability of their slot machine payback statistics; other states have "voluntary" reporting with casinos voluntarily giving these statistics; while still more states and many riverboat cites and Indian reservations have kept their payback statistics shrouded in secrecy. Still, the casino industry is all of a type and you can be fairly certain that as competition grows for the slot dollar, the payback percentages will tend to grow with them. But should you assume that riverboat "A" is returning a decent percentage based upon figures for riverboat "B" in the same general area?

One gaming authority and industry consultant told me this: "In areas where there is competition between riverboats for the same patrons, it's a safe bet to figure you will get similar paybacks. In fact, even in jurisdictions where casinos don't have to publicly reveal their payback statistics, many will advertise them in the local newspapers and magazines to get local players to come to their casinos. Once one casino advertises its slot paybacks, more places jump in and do it. So, you can make a fairly astute guess in a given area, for example dockside riverboats and casinos in Biloxi, Mississippi, that machines of a given denomination will have similar paybacks, give or take a percentage here and there, in the various casinos in that area. It's competition."

So what do the statistics show? Looking at several months to several years of reported statistics for Atlantic City in New Jersey; Las Vegas, Lake Tahoe, Reno and Laughlin in Nevada; and various casinos and riverboats in Colorado, Connecticut, Illinois and Iowa, some general averages and patterns appear that should be of interest to the savvy slot player looking to maximize his or her chances of winning.

Getting a Handle on That Handle

In general, the following "average" patterns are easily recognizable from the statistics that have been publicly reported by the various casinos and gaming commissions:

1. The highest paybacks across the country are on five-dollar or higher machines.

These range from an average high of approximately 97.5 percent in Lake Tahoe, followed by 97 percent for Reno, 96.5 percent for Laughlin and Downtown Las Vegas, to 95.5 percent for casinos on the Las Vegas Strip. Note that Nevada does not break down its statistics by casino, just by area. The Foxwoods casino in Connecticut averages approximately 95 percent on its five-dollar machines, while Atlantic City and Colorado average approximately 94 percent returns on their five-dollar machines. In Atlantic City, the Sands had the highest average paybacks for the statistics I'm citing with a 95.5 percent return, while the Claridge and Resorts had the lowest, approximately 93 percent each.

2. The next highest paybacks are on dollar machines.

Reno had the highest paybacks on dollar machines, averaging approximately a 96 percent return, with all other Nevada venues averaging in the 95 percent range. Colorado casinos averaged approximately 93.5 percent, Foxwoods in Connecticut approximately 92 percent, while Atlantic City averaged approximately 91.5 percent on its dollar machines. In Atlantic City, both Harrah's and Tropworld had the highest paybacks on dollar slots, coming in at approximately 92.5 percent for the statistics studied.

3. The next highest paybacks are on 50-cent machines.

Again Nevada had the best paybacks with downtown Las Vegas averaging approximately 95.5 percent returns, followed by Laughlin with 95 percent, the Las Vegas Strip and Reno with 94 percent and Lake Tahoe with 93 percent. Foxwoods in Connecticut returned approximately 91 percent on 50-cent machines. Atlantic City casinos hover around the 90 percent payback mark with Caesars, Resorts and Tropworld all coming in at approximately 91 percent for their 50-cent machines. No statistics are available for the other cities.

4. Quarter machines come in fourth in percentage of paybacks.

And guess what? Nevada leads the way here also. Downtown Las Vegas with 95.5 percent, Laughlin with 94.5 percent, the Las Vegas Strip and Reno with 94 percent and Lake Tahoe with 93 percent lead the country in 25-cent slot paybacks. Colorado came in at 92 percent. Atlantic City came in around 89.5 percent with Tropworld at 91 percent for high and Caesars at 87.5 percent for low. Foxwoods in Connecticut paid approximately 90 percent on its 25-cent machines.

5. Most venues still have nickel machines and these pay back the lowest percentage.

In Nevada you can expect approximately an 89 percent return; in Colorado you'll find 88.5 percent; in Atlantic City (if you can find them), 83 percent. To make money on smaller-denomination machines the casino has to keep more. It's a space-cost efficiency situation.

6. For almost all multiple-pay and multiple-play machines, regardless of denomination, the maximum coin line tends to yield a better percentage payback.

If you can afford to play maximum coin, do so. However, there is another factor to be aware of and that is this: *Sometimes the maximum number of coin in a lower-denomination machine does not pay back as much as a single coin in a higher-denomination machine.* So if you are playing quarters, read the machine carefully and see if the maximum number of quarters, let's say five, pays back "X"; for a $1.25 investment you are getting "X" return. Now, take a look at what the dollar machine of the same type pays for one dollar. You might find that you are in better shape playing a single dollar on a dollar machine than you are playing maximum coin on the quarter machine because that single dollar will return "X+." This does not always hold true, but it is a consideration when selecting which machine is right for your needs. So watch for it.

7. Generally speaking, the bigger the progressive jackpots, the less the returns on the other winning combinations.

With the giant Megabucks and Quartermania linked-progressive jackpots, it's hard to see the forest for the trees of greed. But the house-edge forest is there, unfortunately, and it's cutting you down with every whack you're taking at that mega jackpot. Although these multi-casino, linked-progressive machines look like the ordinary slots, they are withholding a much greater percentage of the average play in order to pay out the giant jackpots. In short, you are paying with every play for the opportunity to win zillions. Now, unless you hit the big one, you are giving the casino a hefty edge over you when you play giant linked progressives. So, if at all possible, avoid these machines. It's fun to fantasize about winning millions but it is even more fun to actually win a few hundred.

8. Machines in airports, laundromats, bars, novelty stores, drug stores, gas stations and so forth should be avoided at all costs.

There are no industry statistics on how much the machines in the above venue pay back but I have heard estimates as low as 50 percent and as high as 80 percent. My source inside the slot machine industry confirms, however, that machines programmed for such otherwise non-gaming places are programmed to "hold a lot." It is a desperate gambler indeed who plays these machines and one who has no chance of breaking the one-armed bandits. And never, ever, play illegal machines because, illegality aside, what can you expect from machines owned and operated by people who are circumventing the law?

When reading the above statistics, keep in mind that while the patterns will hold from casino to casino, state to state—*the higher the denomination the better the payback, the more coins the better the payback, etc.*—individual casinos or states might increase or decrease their percentage returns at any time for whatever reasons. For example, while the Sands in the statistics I studied had the highest paying five-dollar machines in Atlantic City, by the time you read this, it might have the lowest. I cited the statistics merely to show you a range from casino to casino that exists within a given casino town (when the statistics were available). The fact remains, however, that in the Sands the five-dollar machines will more than likely pay back more than the one-dollar machines, which will pay back more than the 50-cent machines, which will pay back more than the 25-cent machines. The specifics might change but the pattern remains. And this pattern is country-wide!

Interestingly enough, it is not that difficult to find out which casinos or gaming areas are paying back the best returns on their slot machines. Many local and national gaming magazines publish this information. The best publication for the slot player is *The Casino Player Magazine*, published in Atlantic City but covering the entire national gaming scene and available nationwide. Every month *The Casino Player Magazine* charts the recent slot-machine return percentages of the various locales and casinos across the country. So before you decide on where you're going or where you're playing once you get there, it might stand you in good stead to get a current issue of this slick, well-written publication.

The bottom line for slot players is obviously this—if you can afford it—*play the highest denomination machines at the best possible site for that denomination machine and put in the maximum number of coins unless the next highest denomination pays more for the same dollar amount!* That may not be the most poetic line I ever wrote, but it is an accurate single commandment and one you should remember. You'll get the best bang for your buck if you write it on the tablets of your heart.

The Best Machine for You

Now that's fine to say, but if you have only $100 to wager, what would be your best bet—to put that hundred through the five-dollar machine or the one-dollar machine or the 50-cent machine or the 25-cent machine? Theoretically, you would be better off putting it through the five-dollar machine because of its better average payback.

But here's where theory and practice collide head on. If you hit a cold streak on that five-dollar machine, you will be wiped out in no time flat. Of course, if you hit a hot streak, you will make just that much more money. So what to do? That depends on your temperament.

Personally, I wouldn't even consider playing a five-dollar machine if my total gambling capital were $100—especially if I wanted to have that $100 see me through a day or a few days of slot play. Now, if I were a $100 table-game player and I wanted to fool around at the slots for a few minutes, then, yes, I would drop five-dollar coins into the machine and hope for a hit or two because losing that hundred is the equivalent of losing one bet in blackjack or craps or baccarat. No big deal. But it is a BIG deal if that $100 is the "end-all and be-all" of my gambling stake.

I don't know any inveterate slot players who would want to play with such a slim margin of comfort.

And don't be misled by cut-and-dried discussions of probability theory that you might read in gaming books, the first principle for you as a player is to play within your comfort zone. You must be fully prepared psychologically to lose your gambling stake, true, but if you are underfinanced, then you are going to sweat out every decision on the machine because every decision inches you to the brink of ruin. You are going to be extremely uncomfortable in such a case. So you are better off playing nickels if quarters make you sweat, and quarters if 50 cents makes you sweat, and so on. Obviously, you would have to be a Kamikaze slot player to attack a five-dollar machine with a $100 bankroll. Despite the theoretical favorability of the machine compared with its poorer cousins, you are courting rapid economic death by playing this way. So probability theory aside, your best *practical* bet is to always play the denomination of machine that allows you a given amount of predetermined "time" as well as comfort.

Let us say that you want to be able to play the slots for an hour and after that hour you are going home no matter what. You have a $100 bankroll specifically earmarked for playing the slots for that one hour. Let us assume that between putting the coins in and pulling the handle or pressing the button, you can play four decisions a minute (you're a leisurely player), so you want to have enough of a bankroll to get you through 240 decisions in your hour of play. You are not interested in the fact that some, many and, if luck is your lady tonight, most of those decisions will be winners. You want to be confident and comfortable that should you lose every single decision, you will be able to play for that one hour.

Just divide your bankroll into 240 equal shares by dividing it into your $100. So you are able to bet approximately 40 cents per spin (actually 41.66 cents). By playing 40 cents per spin, you have enough to last through your session if the worst disaster befalls you—not a single winner, an unlikely occurrence. (Yes, I know, there aren't many 40-cents-a-spin machines in existence, unless you can find a rare dime machine, but I'm using this simply as an example.)

I guess you can say that a primary principle in breaking the one-armed bandits is not to go broke yourself.

6

The BIG Industry Secret

Where the "LOOSE" Machines
are Located in a Casino!

I've been looking forward to writing this chapter ever since I knew I was going to write this book because, in a very real sense, this chapter is the gambling equivalent to Woodward and Bernstein's expose of the Watergate break-in! (Okay, so I like to dramatically overstate things once in a while.) In all the millions upon millions of words written in books and magazines about the slot machines, one major secret has never been revealed—indeed, no gambling writer has ever discovered an answer to the Big Question: WHERE DO CASINOS PLACE THEIR LOOSE SLOT MACHINES? This has been the BIG industry secret for decades now. And no casino executive, slot manager, or programmer has ever stepped forward and leaked the secret to the public. Why, more secrets have poured out of the White House, the Pentagon, the FBI, the CIA and the boardrooms and bedrooms of the rich and famous than have dripped out about the placement of slot machines in a casino. (I guess you could say that America has its priorities.)

There has been speculation by gaming writers, of course, as to the whereabouts of "loose" machines in a casino; some of it uncannily accurate, some of it bizarre, some of it honest but misinformed, some of it stupid and, perhaps, disingenuous.

Whether executives-in-the-know have been stone-lipped because of loyalty to their establishments, fear of losing their jobs, high moral principles, greed or indifference, the fact remains that no one has been able to get an "insider" to speak honestly and openly about the placement of slot machines inside a casino.

Until now.

My "Deep Throat" is a high-ranking casino executive of a rather large casino company and to get him (her) to reveal his (her) insider information I had to promise him (her) the following:

> 1. That any information I give concerning the casino(s) he's (she's) associated with is given in such a way that the casino(s) cannot be easily identified. Thus, I might be talking about the placement of slots in two or more casinos even as I described it as a "given" casino. Or, I might be actually talking about one casino.

> 2. That I cannot use or profit in any way from the information he (she) gives me (other than writing about it). In other words, I promise not to play the "loose" slots that are being pointed out in his (her) casino(s) or give (or sell) this information to anyone else, including my relatives and friends. (This sounds much more dramatic than it actually is . . . read on.)

> 3. That I keep his (her) identity a secret and that I describe him (her) in such a way as to make identification impossible. [I will from this point always refer to my source as *him* because doing *him (her)* can get to be irritating.]

> 4. That I not reveal his identity to anyone under any circumstances. If brought to court, I must, as a journalist, protect my source. I would call him "Mr. Handle."

> 5. That all tape-recorded conversations be destroyed in his presence after I transcribe his words from the tape to the page—again in his presence.

> 6. That he have final say over the way the material is presented although everything he says to me is "on the record." Mr. Handle was very concerned about "being misquoted or misleading."

I readily agreed to his six requests since they were in no way unusual. Quite a few sources in the gaming world wish to remain anonymous. Some of my best friends prefer anonymity when I quote them or write about their exploits.

As far as my "Deep Throat," or Mr. Handle, was concerned, I only had two stipulations of my own. The first was that the information he gave me be concrete enough to be theoretically of value to slot players looking for "loose" machines— in casinos other than the one(s) he was associated with. So I wanted not only *where* the machines were in his casino(s) but the *reasoning* that went behind putting them there. I wasn't interested in him telling me that some machines are "loose" and others are "tight" and that these "loose" and "tight" machines could be sitting right next to each other. This is common knowledge. I wanted something fresh and new, after all; I wanted something that would give me an insight and a handle that could possibly help my readers select machines in casinos all over the country and thereby dramatically reduce the house edge against them (or, at the very least, be a workable method for selecting machines).

My second stipulation was simple. He had to answer all my questions honestly. Nothing was off-the-record. I wanted to pick his brain. If he didn't know an answer to a question, then fine. There were a few times when I wanted to extrapolate information he gave me based on his casino(s) that could be used in other casinos when he would say that it couldn't be done owing to the different floor arrangements of the casinos. That was fine. I also wanted his insights, even his speculations. After all, he was an expert in how casinos *think*. Knowing how your opponents think is probably the single most important element in planning a strategy against them.

I agreed to his requests. He agreed to mine. We were on.

So have I discovered the "magic bullet" to cure the downtrodden slot player's economic woes? Have I been able to give you an absolute ticket to positive expectation in the world of negative programming? If you could find the exact machines in the exact locations my Deep Throat, Mr. Handle, showed me, would you be *guaranteed* a win? I wish . . . but, unfortunately, the answer is no. There was not one "loose"

machine programmed to pay back 100 (or more) percent in
Mr. Handle's casino(s). There were several 99's and even one
that was scratching on the underbelly of 100 percent. Some
of these loose machines, for short periods of time (as long as
a month), were paying back way over their programming
expectations. Yet, mathematically, Mr. Handle was confident
that all machines would ultimately reflect their programming.
The "loose" machines just showed more positive fluctuations
(for the player) than the tight ones. This was to be *expected*,
actually.

However, without question, more players went home
winners on the "loose" machines than on the tight ones—especially players who played for a couple of days or more. Still
more players were actually able, with comps factored in with
relatively small losses, to show a profit over an extended period of time on the "loose" machines. Indeed, on the 99 percenters, long-term play plus a full range of comps seemed to
be an almost break-even proposition! Not bad at all!

Now meet my "Deep Throat," Mr. Handle, so dubbed in
honor of the one-armed bandits he's unmasking—and get
ready to be in on the top's secrets!

Frank: So where are the "loose" machines?

Mr. Handle (*laughing*): Nothing like coming right to the
point! Maybe I should define what I mean, or rather,
what a casino might mean, when we characterize machines as "loose." So we have a common . . . a common
concept of what we mean and what we're talking about.

Frank: A common frame of reference for interviewer, inter-
viewee and reader. Let's get the terms straight. Fine.

Mr. Handle: Right. "Loose" refers to machines that are programmed to pay back a greater percentage of the total
monies played than are other machines of a similar kind
or just other machines in your particular casino(s). So
when I say loose machines I mean these machines. In
some casinos a loose machine might be one programmed
at 93 percent return, but in another casino a loose ma-

chine could be 97 or 98. Loose is a relative term, not an absolute term. What's loose for one casino could be tight for another. Loose doesn't mean that the machine is programmed to give the player an edge or anything like that.

Also, I am talking about *programming* and not actual *performance*. When you glance at a spread sheet of actual performance statistics for any given machine or carousel or group of machines, for a day, a week, a month, you will see deviations from the programming norm. Sometimes the deviations are quite large, particularly for a single machine—especially in short-term analysis, a day or a week, or if a big jackpot was paid out recently, the deviation will be great. The reverse is true, too. If a jackpot hasn't been hit in a long, long time, the machine will appear to be holding back much more than its programming. So performance and programming are not the same thing.

Frank: But in the long run the performance of the machine will ultimately reflect its programming?

Mr. Handle: Within a few decimal points, yes, most of the time it will.

Frank: Do you have a workable idea of what you mean by the long run?

Mr. Handle: Depends on the machine's total probabilities. Although I'm versed in math, I'm not a mathematician, or a programmer for that matter. However, if you had 8,000 possible combinations and at the end of one million pulls you were not seeing results consistent with the programming of the machine, not exactly reflecting the programming but at least within a decent range of it, you might look into the machine to see if something's wrong. Also, quite a bit depends on the type of machine. For example, Megabucks or any huge progressive that is linked with other casinos, you're talking about millions of possibilities but you're also talking about thousands of machines all linked. So it gets pretty complicated trying to give an exact number for the long run.

Frank: So you want to see the program reflected in your statistics after a certain length of time even though the statistics and the programming at any given time won't be a perfect match?

Mr. Handle: Correct. You want to see the shadow on the wall. That shadow should be in the shape of the programming.

Frank: For the purposes of our discussion, in your specific casino(s) how do you define "loose?" Give me some real percentages.

Mr. Handle: The "loose" range for us is 97, 98 and 99 percent for a given type of machine. The mid-range is 94, 95 and 96. The low end is 83 to 93—these are our "tight" machines. We have more "loose" machines in the dollar or higher than we do in the quarter category, although in all categories except nickels the mid-range dominates.

Frank: Take the dollar machines. Of a hundred machines, what percentage are programmed loose, mid-range and tight?

Mr. Handle: Ten loose, 60 mid-range, 30 tight.

Frank: On the quarter and nickel machines?

Mr. Handle: Five loose, 55 mid-range, 40 tight on the quarters. We don't have loose nickel machines at all. Eighty percent would be in the tight range with a big tilt toward the lower end of that range.

Frank: Of the loose category of dollar machines, what percentage would be at 99?

Mr. Handle: Given ten machines in the loose category?

Frank: Yes.

Mr. Handle: A half a machine at best would be in the 99 percentage range. Eight of the machines would be 97 percent and one and one-half machine would be 98 percent.

Frank: Let's go to the original question. Where are the loose machines located?

Mr. Handle: The loosest machines, our 99 percenters, are located at what we call the slot crosswalks, or slot squares. These are areas that are readily visible from other slot banks and also areas that slot players walk through. The 99 percenters are machines that can handle a small crowd gathering to watch a person play. They are never in the middle of a row of machines. They are used as lures for other slot players to motivate them to play. We want someone to be sitting at one of these machines, hitting and hitting, and we want others to see or hear what's happening. Our 99 percenters are also programmed to hit the big ones more often. This is a psychological plus for slot players. When they hear someone screaming and they look up and they can see from where they're playing someone at one of the slot crosswalks overwhelmed with joy at winning a jackpot, well, that encourages them to keep right on playing.

The greatest incentive for slot players to play is seeing and hearing other slot players winning because they feel that next time it will be them. So our loosest machines are used as a lure for increasing the slot play of others on our other machines.

Frank: Are you telling me that the old idea that the loosest machines are by doorways and aisles is correct?

Mr. Handle: No. Slot crosswalks or slot squares are not necessarily near doors to the street or near the show lines or near the table-game area—especially not near the table-game area. The crosswalks are the areas where slot players walk to go from bank to bank within the slot areas. The squares are areas, small areas with just a few machines in a thoroughfare, where slot players walk from aisle to aisle. They are usually a single machine or a small or perhaps round bank of machines that are visible from many vantage points within the longer rows or banks of slot machines. These machines can even be elevated. They are highly visible from many vantage points within the slot playing areas.

Frank: And they get heavy play?

Mr. Handle: On the weekends, when it's more crowded, they get good action—which is really when we want them to be played. During the week, people can spread out in the slot areas. Get comfortable. So they aren't looking to sit in view of other people or feel the need to stretch out because they're cramped by other slot players. So you won't see these 99 percenters getting quite that much action mid-week. But on the weekends the traffic is pretty heavy in the slot aisles. People aren't quite as relaxed. So we want two things to happen. We want some people to play the machines that are in the crosswalks and squares and we want other people to be motivated enough to put up with some of the crowds in the slot aisles. So the crowds push people onto the 99 percenters and the 99 percenters, as they hit more often, motivate the other players to continue playing even if it's a little crowded in their aisles. Also, a person at a tight machine will keep pumping coins in when he sees someone at a loose machine winning. It's an incentive to keep playing.

Frank: So "loose" machines aren't placed at the end of aisles and near doorways as the popular wisdom states?

Mr. Handle: Mid-range machines are near access doors or areas because mid-range machines will keep patrons sitting and we want people to see other people playing our machines. But the really "loose" machines are placed to encourage people already playing to continue to play or to play two or more machines. We want slot players to see other slot players winning so the loosest machines will always be visible from many slot-playing vantage points.

Frank: So one of my readers goes to your casino(s) and checks out different banks of machines. From each bank in a given area, he can see a certain machine or a couple of machines. He goes here and he goes there and he sees that machine.

Mr. Handle: And that will most likely be the 99 percenter!

Frank: And the 98 percenters?

Mr. Handle: Same basic situation. We would set up the 98 percenters in small banks or carousels that would be highly visible from other adjoining slot areas. These groupings would look like any other grouping except that they would have more visibility from the other banks.

Frank: So your "loose" machines are never to be found in the regular aisles or banks of slots?

Mr. Handle: Oh, no, we certainly do sprinkle "loose" machines in our banks of slots, but never the 99 percenters. Especially on the weekends, you want some people in each row to be winning some jackpots. That reinforces play. You have someone near you winning, maybe on the machine right next to you and you have someone in a crosswalk winning. And someone in the aisle behind you and on the next aisle over and so forth. It generates excitement hearing all those coins falling into the hopper. Also a loose machine will give the player playing it the incentive to play the very, very tight machine right next to him. So what one machine might pay out, in the long run the other machine is taking. That's almost an ironclad law that you will have a very tight machine next to a very loose machine.

Frank: Where else would you place loose machines?

Mr. Handle: Near certain change booths. You'll notice something interesting mid-week, at least in my casino(s). Many of the more public locations—as I already said, the crosswalks and squares—but also the machines near change booths, don't get very heavy action. But on the weekends when the casino is jumping, people are forced by the crowds to play these machines. Now, the larger crowds also mean a longer wait for individuals getting change at a booth or cashing in coupons. So while these people wait to get their money, the machines near them are hitting. It gets them revved up to play. They won't necessarily play the machines they are watching or hearing, but they will be charged up to go into the machine banks, select a machine and play on. They might also be motivated to buy more coins as they see winners. Again, machines near change booths afford great visibility for winners, the people on line, people walking by, people on other machines in the surrounding area. And those winners encourage more playing by others. Thus, it makes sense to populate those areas with loose machines as an incentive to slot players to get into or continue on with the action.

Frank: So where are the tight machines?

Mr. Handle: The tightest machines in my casino(s) are all surrounding the table-game pits.

Frank: That goes against some of the popular wisdom.

Mr. Handle: Definitely and on purpose. Our 83-percent machines surround the table-game area and we have good reasons for doing this. Most table-game players like to drop some silver in the machines as they walk by either before or usually after they play at the tables. Some quarters sometimes and at other times some dollars. Most table-game players are not going to be crushed if they lose those few coins. If they do win, most table-game players just take their winnings. They aren't motivated as are slot players to keep playing. So why reward them? So all the end machines in the table-game area are at 83 percent and when the table players drop a few coins in them we get a good hold on them. More table-game players have read books on gambling than have slot players and most of them know about the idea that end machines are loose. Well, not the end machines in the table-game area!

Also, table-game players aren't going to stop playing blackjack or craps to gather round a big slot winner—they'll just look over their shoulders—and they aren't going to run and start playing coins. In fact, we wouldn't want to see play suddenly stop or pause at the tables because some slot player hit a jackpot. Table-game players wouldn't be motivated to play slots by the win anyway—so why give them an opportunity to stop or pause in their playing? That's another reason why the tight machines are placed around the table-game area. A pause in the table action is money we aren't winning from the players at the tables, after all.

Frank: Does the same hold true for the machines by the show line or food lines?

Mr. Handle: Yes and no. The show-line end machines are tight because other than when there's a show they get very little play and like the table-game area, whatever coins are played in them are casual, whatever a person has in his pocket or her purse. There's no commitment to play and no real expectation of winning and no negative feelings when those few coins are lost. However, banks of machines near the coffee shop would be in the upper mid-range with here and there a very good sprinkling of loose machines because as slot players eat they will hear up close the sounds of winning. So as they eat, their motivation to play builds up. So those banks of machines by a coffee shop would be a good bet for finding loose machines.

Frank: So let me just tick off what we have for a minute. Highly visible machines from many angles and vantage points are loose . . .

Mr. Handle: In slot areas. Remember these visible machines are for slot players in the slot areas. It doesn't matter if the machines are visible from the sports book or the table game area. Its visibility from other slot banks—that is the criteria. We want slot players to be super motivated.

Frank: Near entrances or doors you will find mid-range machines. Tight ones surround the table game areas and show lines. Mid-range and loose machines by the coffee shop area.

Mr. Handle: Yes. Of course, some casinos don't have their coffee shops near any machines so this wouldn't apply to them . . . obviously.

Frank: Now what about the placement of machines in the actual slot aisles. Do you have some kind of predetermined order like loose, tight, tight, loose, tight, mid range, mid range and so on?

Mr. Handle: Yes, but it varies widely depending on where the particular bank of machines is located. Remember that all placement decisions have been made with a single philosophy in mind—encouraging more slot play and increasing the slot play of the people currently at the machines.

Frank: Well, give me some "for examples." For example, the table-game area, machines near the table-game area. Give me a placement pattern for these machines first.

Mr. Handle: Okay. Let's say that the machines touch the table-game area at 90 degree angles, which is usual. Now, here is our rule of thumb: A table-game player casually walking by will play one of the first three machines. Three deep is about as far as a tall person can reach in to put a few coins in a machine or as far as anyone would go into a bank just to play a couple of quarters or dollars before moving on. So those first three machines will be tight, with the tightest being the end one. Also, if the table game player has to walk through a given slot aisle to get to the elevators or to the outside, the machines in that aisle will be tight ones.

Here's another aspect to consider. Table-game players are not energized by the noise from the slot areas as are slot players. They don't particularly like the sound of coins falling into trays. If that sound is in the distance then that's okay but not right up close. Smaller casinos don't have the luxury of what I'm talking about, but in bigger casinos where slot play by the table-game area is somewhat slower compared to other areas, why annoy your table-game players if you don't have to? It's a secondary consideration but a consideration nevertheless. So let the slot noise be in the background for the table-game players.

Frank: And let it be in the foreground for slot players?

Mr. Handle: That's it. Let winning machines be where slot players congregate. Where feasible, that would be the placement philosophy. Now, the fourth machine in from the table-game area would be mid-range interspersed with tight. A second bank or row away from the table-game area and things would change however, and you would start seeing mid-range almost exclusively with here and there "loose" and "tight" machines. We would not put two loose machines side by side or even every other one. A general guideline is that loose machines in slot banks are at least four machines apart, but preferably one loose machine per 12 and three tight machines per 12 in the slot areas with the rest mid-range. That's a general placement profile.

Frank: How accurate would this be for other casinos?

Mr. Handle: Fairly accurate, I would guess. It's hard to say exactly, but casinos of similar sizes basically do the same things for the same reasons. I would be very surprised to see slot machines abutting table-game areas programmed to pay out the highest percentages in a given casino. I don't think that would be a successful placement policy.

Frank: In craps there's a superstition concerning "weekend dice." That on weekends the casinos use a different kind of cube that makes the seven come up. So far as I'm able to tell there is no truth to this superstition. How about "weekend machines?" Do you reprogram machines on the weekends to be tighter? Or are machines reprogrammed during the day to make them tight or loose at night or anything like that?

Mr. Handle: No, that would be impossible. It's also not necessary. A casino has its machines programmed in advance to reflect its marketing philosophy and how much action they expect, how much of a total return they expect to give. So we're looking at a total picture. On a weekend you might see us holding more because more players are playing. This causes tight machines, for example, in the table game area, on weekends to get much heavier play than they normally would on the weekdays. Since there are more tight machines than loose machines, more play would inevitably give us more money. But programming and reprogramming machines would be silly and not necessary and a waste of time.

Frank: Do you steer Big Players to better-paying machines?

Mr. Handle: Do we have the same definition of "Big Player?"

Frank: I don't know. Give me your definition of "Big Player" as it relates to slots.

Mr. Handle: In slots, as in table games, it's essentially time and money and casino advantage factored in to get a profile. How much time a player puts in at a machine, actually how many decisions or pulls of the handle, multiplied by how much money he plays. So if a player plays at a five-dollar machine for four hours that's worth more to us than a player playing at a quarter machine for that length of time. Even though our five-dollar machines are programmed to give back more than our quarter machines, we will win more from a five-dollar player just from sheer dollar figures. A given number of decisions at the quarter machines against the same number of decisions at the five-dollar machines will yield us a smaller percentage profit but a greater actual profit owing to the large denomination being played. And remember that a five-dollar machine and a quarter machine of the same type take up the same amount of space in the casino. So whichever machine is returning to us a greater real amount for its floor space requirements is the machine we're most interested in. Or, rather, the player playing that machine is the player we're most interested in.

Frank: This is an ironic thing when you consider it. It's better for the player to play the highest denomination machine he can afford because the casino cut is less. Yet it's better for the casino too because in actual fact, that cut is more money for the casino.

Mr. Handle: Yes. And what's more, a five-dollar-machine player will get better comps too. So the bigger the player, the better for us and for the player. Also, the five-dollar players over time have more winning sessions. So it's good for both the casino and the player.

Frank: Always assuming the player can afford that level of play.

Mr. Handle: Yes.

Frank: Okay, do you have five-dollar machines returning 99 percent?

Mr. Handle: No. In fact, the programming for all our five-dollar machines falls exactly in the same range—95, 96, 97 and 98 percent. There is no particular placement philosophy and all machines are interspersed, although we have more 95 percent machines than 98, as you would expect.

Frank: Essentially because they are all paying back a relatively loose rate and also because you have comparatively fewer machines and players?

Mr. Handle: Yes. Also, a five-dollar player is a five-dollar player. At that level and higher, the player has conditioned himself or has been conditioned by the better payouts and comps to continue to play at this level. We really don't have to do anything to stimulate a five-dollar player's appetite. We are also finding that in recent years more players are playing these five-dollar machines. In years gone by, you didn't get much action on a machine of this denomination. It was more a conversation piece. Today, it is the preferred machine for many players.

Frank: The five-dollar players don't have to be lured into playing for longer hours or more money?

Mr. Handle: Correct. Generally, our five-dollar or higher players are very consistent in terms of hours played and so forth.

Frank: Continue with the definition of Big Player as it applies to dollar machines or even quarter machines.

Mr. Handle: A dollar player, a quarter player or a nickel player is rated just the same way as a five-dollar or higher player. In a nutshell, how much total money has the individual put through the machines in his playing time and what theoretical edge do we have over that money? We are willing to give back a certain percentage of an individual's slot play in the form of comps . . .

Frank: What percentage?

Mr. Handle: Forty percent of the theoretical loss, more or less. The 40 percent for the five-dollar player will have a greater monetary value than for a dollar player for the same amount of play. Or you can figure it another way, that we'll return one percent or a little less of the total amount of the money played in the form of comps. Casinos can figure it either way. Most slot clubs return a fixed percentage of total play. This is computerized. However, a host would handle a big player based on our percentage over him.

Frank: So if you could consistently play a 99 percenter, and were returned one percent of your total play, you would be theoretically able to break even?

Mr. Handle: Yes.

Frank: Let's look at a Big Player another way. The same way a casino rates him at a table game, by returning a percent of the theoretical edge over the player. You said 40 percent more or less of your theoretical hold on a big player? Give me an example of more, give me an example of less. I want to know how your judgment comes in on this.

Mr. Handle: More would be someone who comes quite frequently, perhaps with a spouse, perhaps with friends, and can be relied on to give us good play over extended periods of time. Less would be someone, usually on the weekend, who might not be a regular—comes once or twice a year. Of course, many casinos now have gone to computerized slot clubs and this has made it easy for us. Everything is computerized and the player is given points for his play and these points are redeemable for comps. But some decisions still have to be made by casino hosts—do you give Mr. X a room for a certain night and so forth.

Frank: So joining a slot club is essential for a player?

Mr. Handle: Yes, especially in the bigger casinos and especially if you aren't a huge player.

Frank: What about the practice of steering?

Mr. Handle: You mean purposefully showing a preferred player a loose machine?

Frank: Yes.

Mr. Handle: Do you think that would be ethical?

Frank: You have the edge on every machine. You've got a Big Player who has dropped quite a bit of money. I don't know. You tell him play that machine over there, I think it's a hot one. Of course, you know it's one of your 99 per-centers. Would something like that be a common practice?

Mr. Handle (*laughing*): And then he comes back to that machine for the rest of his life and we give him one percent of his action in the form of comps and he breaks even and we lose the revenue from a previously "good" player?

Frank: That could be a problem, for you. Nice for him though.

Mr. Handle: Formally, we have a rule that no one—that includes change personnel, floor people, hosts, anyone connected with the casino—no one can offer advice as to which machine should be played.

Frank: But?

Mr. Handle: Well, it's no secret that some slot players go to the change people and ask their advice and that the change people sometimes offer an "informed" opinion as to which machines are likely to get hot.

Frank: You said "informed" sarcastically. You don't think some of your personnel have figured out at least some elements of your placement?

Mr. Handle: I don't really think so. Remember that our placement is done with long-term goals in mind. Those tight machines could be hitting quite often on a given night. I think you would really have to study the machines over an extended period of time to actually see the pattern that we've created. A change person who had done that would probably not have had time to give change, she would have had to observe for her shift.

Frank: If she did observe, would she be able to get a sense of placement? What about just a sense of where the loose

machines were because over the months of her employ-
ment she's witnessed so many wins on them that consciously or unconsciously she knows these machines to
be good? Not that she's actively studied them but over
time, she's realized that, hey, those machines over by the
change booth seem to pay back more often than those
machines over by the table games?

Mr. Handle: Perhaps. Yes, I guess that would be possible. However, in the real world, I think most change people don't
know where the loose machines are and if they give advice it is merely to get tips should the patron hit a big one.

Frank: What about you personally? Would you ever steer a
preferred player to better-paying machines?

Mr. Handle: Well . . . not in so many words. I might say
something to the effect "Have you tried the machines in
that area?"—knowing that they contain a high number
of loose or mid-range machines. I wouldn't ever select
or steer to a single machine. And I don't think I'd even
casually steer someone to a 99 percenter.

Frank: So you would gently steer?

Mr. Handle: Yes, perhaps, to an area but not a machine per
se. And, again, not a 99 percenter.

Frank: What about out-and-out moving of machines? You have
some of your preferred customers in a given area week
after week and you decide to reward them by moving in
some loose machines just like the type they like to play
only paying back 97 or 98 percent. Would you do that?

Mr. Handle: No.

Frank: Have you ever heard of this practice?

Mr. Handle: Yes. But it would be stupid to do. A waste of
time. It's one thing to say to a preferred player, try those

machines over there, it's quite another to move the machines in a casino around.

Frank: But you have heard of the practice?

Mr. Handle: Yes. But I've heard of many practices, mostly fictitious, I'll tell you. I think the rumor started because every once in a while we do change the arrangement of our machines. This is done for practical purposes. We're reorganizing a given area to include more machines in the same space, or where looking to get more visibility for our loose machines. But we wouldn't go through the hassle of moving machines around to help out a player. Moving banks of machines around is a huge undertaking.

Frank: Okay, I notice that the real placement philosophy you cite is totally wrapped up in the psychological aspects of gaming. The placement of machines is done to encourage play or increasing the total hours of play by people who already play the slots.

Mr. Handle: That's it, really.

Frank: How do you encourage non-slot players to play?

Mr. Handle: It's not too much of a problem really. New gamblers almost invariably wind up playing the slot machines because the table games can be intimidating. With the growth of casino gaming there has been a growth in the total number and total percentages of slot players compared to table-game players. This is inevitable. New gamblers go to the area that affords them the least stress—that's slots. Of course, we do market our slots heavily. It's the dream of winning the big jackpots. So our advertisements and mailings promote the slots heavily and we're always sending press releases out with pictures of the winners and so on. But the slot movement is overwhelming. I would estimate that eight or nine of every 10 new casino players are slot players. Winning big jackpots is the stuff of dreams and casinos are in the business of catering to dreams.

Frank: So it's not the Age of Aquarius, it's the age of slots?

Mr. Handle: Good point.

Frank: What about the so-called specialty machines? Are any of these worth playing?

Mr. Handle: Well, certainly video poker is a great game, if you know the right strategies to employ.

Frank: My next book will cover all the video poker strategies and how to find full-pay machines.

Mr. Handle: You can even get a slight edge on some machines but you won't find that many of those machines.

Frank: You have to know what to look for and how to play it once you find it. Yes, but what about other specialty machines aside from video poker? What we would define as non-skilled machines, because certainly video poker is much like blackjack, a combination of skill and luck.

Mr. Handle: Most of our other machines are singletons or we might have a few machines of a given type. Machines like the pony races, or Derby, the coin pushers and the like. These machines aren't really big money makers for us, except for video keno, which has a remarkably big following.

Frank: If they aren't big money makers for you, does that mean the players are getting a good shake from them?

Mr. Handle: No. We have a big percentage on these machines—all of them can be considered tight. It's just that they don't get that much play so we don't make much off them.

Frank: So it would be a safe bet that except for specific skill games such as video poker and some video-blackjack games . . . it would be a safe bet to say that you should avoid all specialty or novelty games?

Mr. Handle: Well, from the casinos' point of view, we'd like players to spend all their playing time on these machines. But seriously, they aren't the best bets available from the players' point of view. In our casino(s) these games are there more to break up the landscape than anything else. I would assume that elsewhere it would be the same—you get a better game on the regular slots, yes.

Frank: You've been quite instructive and I think that many of your points are transferrable to other casinos. I think my readers will be helped.

Mr. Handle: Even if some of my placement information isn't transferrable, I don't think it would hurt keeping this information in the back of your mind when you go to a casino to play the slots. If you walk into a casino and by blind chance select a machine, well, that's about the worst case. You can't do any worse by using the information I've given.

Frank: And you can do better. It can't hurt and it can only help is what you're saying.

Mr. Handle: Yes, exactly. Of course, no matter what, the player isn't going to get the edge on us—even if we had signs pointing out the loosest machines in the casino. That's a given.

Frank: Except, perhaps, some video-poker games and 99 percenters with a one percent comp return.

Mr. Handle: You'd have to really know your stuff for video poker.

Frank: Only one real question remains to be asked and answered. Why are you telling me these things? Why have you agreed to speak to me about the slots honestly? I've spoken to many casino executives about slots and about other aspects of gambling over the years. They have been a very reticent group, to say the least. More often than not, you get the run-around. The answers are vague or given as if by rote. Yet here you are being as specific as you can be. So, why?

Mr. Handle: The casino industry is a very paranoid industry. Jobs are not secure on any level and almost everyone is almost always worried about losing his or her job. And many of my colleagues are suspicious and frightened of the press. We want to control the flow of information in the media and not leave ourselves open. Also, I know many people in the industry who have been hurt by bad publicity—professionally and personally. Even though gaming is growing incredibly in this country, there's still a stigma attached to it. After all, we are in the business of taking people's money, no matter how nicely you phrase it. The majority of the people on any given night in a casino are losing and the overwhelming majority in any given stretch of time are losing their money to us. Just about every expose of the casino industry makes us out to be bandits—if not completely controlled by organized crime, then certainly co-conspirators. And you always see stories about some poor soul with a gambling problem losing every penny he has—so is it any wonder why casino executives don't want to open up to the press?

Frank: But you did . . . why?

Mr. Handle: First of all . . . no, let me get to the heart of why I gave you this information. *I really don't know.* How's that for an answer? I'm not quite sure of why I'm doing this. I wish I could say that I'm doing it for some noble reason. To help my fellow man and all, but that isn't why. I really don't know why. I do know that nothing I've revealed can hurt my casino(s) because how many people are going to read your book—no offense. How many of the people who do read your book are going to come into my particular casino(s) on a steady enough basis to hurt us? No one. On the weekends, the 99 percenters are always busy anyway—so it might be someone who read your book playing on them instead of someone just stumbling upon them by chance. And in fact, I think your book will actually help us—let us say you sell a million copies . . .

Frank: If we're fantasizing let's say 10 million.

Mr. Handle: Okay. Those people will want to play. Maybe they figure they will have a better chance against us now that they have some good information. So instead of coming once a year, they come four times a year. And, in fact, your book does give them a better chance, but still we take a smaller cut over a longer run and over a bigger population so we make our profits no matter what. It's good for everyone, I guess.

But I wish I could say I had some noble reason for telling you the inside scoop on the placement of machines. I actually don't. I'm not paranoid and I really don't see the casino industry toppling because your readers might make out better than the average players. And in the years to come everyone will want to know who was this "Mr. Handle" who told the secrets of slot placement, and only you and I will ever know.

Summation

Mr. Handle has given us valuable information. Perhaps the most optimistic conclusion we can draw from his revelations is that it is theoretically possible on a 99-percent machine to have an even game against the house—if we factor in a one-percent comp bonus for sustained play. That means you have to hunt for those loose machines. So let's summarize where you are most likely to find them and most likely not to find them.

The five areas where the "loose" machines will most likely be found:

1. Outside the coffee shop.

2. Near the change booths.

3. In slot aisles or crosswalks.

4. On elevated carousels.

5. At highly visible locations from other slot aisles.

The five areas where the "tight" machines will most likely be found:

1. The aisles of slots surrounding the table-game area.

2. The aisles that table-game players use to get to the elevators or to the outside.

3. Near the show lines and ticket lines.

4. Highly visible machines from the racing and sports books.

5. Highly visible machines from the table-game area.

7

My Personal Observations

in the Wonderland of Slots

After several hours of conversations with Mr. Handle, I decided to tour his casino(s) on my own to get a feel for what he had told me. In addition, I wanted to see with my own eyes how a person could select slots based upon his information. Would, for example, tight slots in the 83 percent range, after several hours of observation, be distinguishable from the loose slots? Using Mr. Handle's information as a general guide to locating better-paying machines, would a player actually be able to fix upon a loose one? Was it possible that the information he had given me was theoretically accurate but practically useless—unless, like me, you knew the exact machines that were loose in the casino?

My instincts told me that a 98 or 99 percenter should be readily distinguishable from an 83 percenter during a two-hour period of steady play. My logic told me that two hours or ten hours might not be enough to separate the slot wheat from the slot chaff. Of course, knowing the specific locations of the loose and tight machines inside Mr. Handle's casino(s) could be a boon or a detriment. Would I imagine the loose machines paying more during the short run simply because I knew them to be loose? Would I perceive the tight machines as stingy during this same time even if they were actually paying more? In short, was I programming myself to see what I expected to see? Would I be able to see the pattern that Mr. Handle talked about? The only thing to do was to observe for a prolonged period of time.

I also had another point I wanted to ascertain. Would loose machines be played more by "regulars"? I defined regulars as anyone who played several times a week at the casino(s). Would these regulars, by a natural-selection process, have stumbled on the looser machines? In the back of my mind I had a little theory I was working on.

Then I figured, why not just get my four researchers and take detailed notes and do several hundred interviews over an extended period of time? But when I asked Mr. Handle about such a thing, he felt that would draw too much attention to me since I would be focusing on specific machines that he had told me about. Too obvious, he said. He also felt that this would disturb slot players who, more often than not, were looking to relax and not chatter as they played—especially not chatter to someone taking copious notes of their every word.

I reluctantly agreed.

In addition, several days earlier one of my researchers, who was helping me take a survey of slot players' attitudes at a Las Vegas Strip casino, was surrounded by security guards and whisked into the back room where, needless to say, she had to explain herself. That little incident embarrassed and upset her. In a casino, it's one thing to stand at a roulette wheel or craps table and record numbers, but it's quite another to be doing massive, formal research—unless it's for something the casino wants researched.

Instead, I decided to make a two-day, three- and four-session-per-day informal study. I would take a Wednesday and Saturday and watch for three discreet two-hour periods on Wednesday: one in the late morning, one in the afternoon and one in the evening. On Saturday, I'd include a fourth period—after midnight. I would walk through the casino, watch players at the various machines, see if one could distinguish by observation which machines were which and whether regulars, if and when they played, had found the better machines based on a natural-selection principle.

I decided to write my results in diary form after every observation. This was not difficult. I just went over to the cocktail lounge and rapidly jotted down what I had witnessed. Although I didn't do formal interviews, or give out survey sheets (as my researchers and I did at other locations), I did talk to people casually. What I found was interesting, enlightening, and I believe it will be useful. I will give you my diary entries (in a slightly more literate form than I actually made them) and then draw some conclusions from my observations.

Wednesday: 11 AM–1 PM

The casino had more people in it than I expected. First, I went to the bank of machines by the coffee shop. They were getting fairly heavy play. From the looks on their faces, the players all seemed rather content. In fifteen minutes of watching, no one left her machine (all the players happened to be women). These were loose and mid-range machines and that would probably explain why there wasn't much movement on the part of players. If they were getting a good return that would keep them playing.

I casually asked one woman why she played that particular machine. She stated: "I've always had good luck over here."

I asked her if she played here a lot. She said two or three times a week—and always at these machines. Some of the other women I talked to also played these machines but were not as clear as to why. One just said: "I don't know. I like these over here."

Next, I walked over to the table-game area. Stayed there for about 20 minutes. Checked out each row of machines that started in the table-game area (most at that 90 degree angle to the table-game pits). They were getting only sporadic play. Once or twice someone would walk by and drop a few coins in an end machine. I saw only one winner and he pocketed his small win and moved on. This reflected what Mr. Handle had said about the type of play you get on the end machines in the table-game area.

Then I journeyed into the banks of machines as far from the table-game area as I could get. Sure enough, there were small, sometimes round, sometimes elevated carousels of highly visible machines. I walked around and sat down in the slot aisles—yes, these certain machines and groups of machines could be seen from many different vantage points within the slot areas. I was beginning to think of these machines as the "visible" machines, which is what I'll call them from now on. These would be the loose ones, many of which were programmed to return 99 percent. Strangely enough, many of them were being played. Mr. Handle had said they didn't get as much action during the week but it seemed to me that they were.

I talked to a few people at these machines—they were all regulars, people who played daily for a few minutes or hours, or three or four times a week, always in the mornings or afternoons. Universally, they said that these were their favorite machines. Without the players actually saying it, I got the distinct impression that the morning regulars at the visible machines intuitively knew they were at good machines—and were somewhat reticent to recommend them to me (or anyone) because they didn't want anyone moving in on their golden goose. That's the impression I got, anyway.

I checked the regular slot aisles. Here people spaced themselves out. Player, empty machine, empty machine, player, empty machine, empty machine and so forth. It seemed that whenever possible people preferred to spread out.

Went to the table-game area again—to listen. In the distance were the sounds of coins hitting trays. Here and there. An intermittent background. A faint echo.

Then I went back into the slot aisles and the coins hitting trays seemed much louder, although again only here and there. In my two hours there were several screams of people who had won jackpots. I walked over; most were on mid-range machines.

By 12:30, the coffee shop had a good-sized crowd. I sat down to have a salad and to listen. The sounds of coins hitting trays were quite noticeable. It seemed that every few seconds someone was winning something on the machines just outside the coffee shop. When I finished my salad I walked around these machines—just about all of them had people playing them. Many of the same people I had seen earlier were still here two hours later.

Wednesday: 4 PM to 6 PM

Decided to make the same circuit as in earlier reconnoitering. Slot machines by the coffee shop were jam-packed. No familiar faces from the morning. Talked to about a dozen people—most were regulars—some were tourists but they only played here when they played this particular casino. A couple just picked these machines at random but these did not consider themselves regulars. They seemed a little stunned that I even talked to them. Some people are very intense when they're playing and when I said something to them they jumped.

Several of the regular ladies volunteered that they thought these machines were "hotter" more often than others they had played. They were right. The women who said this were at machines that were returning approximately 98 percent.

One lady said that she had won her biggest jackpot over here and that people "even came out of the restaurant [coffee shop] to watch!"

I asked some of the regulars if they were up overall in their slot playing careers. None were. Yet all seemed happy to play. Some cited the fact that there was more room in this particular area than in the other slot areas and thus it was more comfortable.

Went to the table-game area at five o'clock, having spent an hour with the "coffee-shop crowd," as I'm beginning to think of the players who play there.

The tables were pretty full. A lively craps game was in progress. The machines around the table-game area were getting more play than in the morning. I just watched for half an hour. There was more movement in this area than at the coffee shop. Didn't notice it at first, then it hit me. More people left machines faster than they did at the coffee shop. The end machines— actually the end three machines—of each row got very little sustained play but some table players dropped some coins in every so often while I watched. None won. Also, none of the table-game players sat for any length of time. They were just dropping some coins and moving on.

In the aisles far from the table games was the same spreading-out phenomena I had witnessed earlier in the day. There were more people playing so it was usually a player, empty machine, player, empty machine, empty machine, player, empty machine, player and so forth. Mr. Handle had mentioned that you could not expect to find loose machines side by side in these slot aisles. Usually, one of every four machines, more often one in 12 or more. The noise in the slot areas was much greater than in the table-game area—were the ceilings different? Did sound bounce more off machines? Of course, there were more machines hitting because there were more players playing.

Just before I left, I went over to the change booths. More people playing here too. Looked into some trays—some were overflowing. Buy-ins or wins? Talked to some of the winners. Most were playing here because it was too crowded in the aisles.

Noticed throughout my journey into the slot areas that the visible machines were getting about the same play as in the morning—maybe even a little less. Hmmmm? Were the morning players better at selecting machines?

Asked several players on the loose machines why they had selected these machines. Half of the ones I talked to said they played these machines "all the time." The other half had no particular reason for doing so.

I should remember to make mention of the fact that I wasn't all that interested in the denomination being played—I was observing quarter machines and dollar machines about equally. Occasionally took a glance at the five-dollar machines. Only a few people at the five-dollar machines. No one was playing the higher denominations. All well-coiffured women at the five-dollar machines, however. I didn't notice much difference between the quarter and dollar slots, actually, but a few percentage points in such short-term observations wouldn't be noticeable anyway.

Wednesday: 9 PM to 11 PM

The place is really crowded. Amazing how many people come to casinos on a Wednesday night. Took my regular route. First stop, the coffee shop. Packed. Just about every machine was being played. Heard a lot of coins hitting trays. At this particular casino, great care has been taken to situate the slots near the coffee shop so as to give the dining patrons a greater "clang" for their bucks. Bad pun, but it's appropriate.

The players were almost evenly divided between men and women, whereas earlier sessions were heavily weighted in favor of the women. Asked a change girl: "Are these good machines?" She said they were. When I went over to the table-game area, I asked a change girl the same question. She shrugged and said she had no idea because she had just started working there a few months ago and "anyway, we aren't supposed to talk about the machines, just give change."

At the coffee-shop area several people hit for fairly decent jackpots in a half hour. When the shouts of the winners were heard, people came over to see what was up. There's plenty of room in this area for small crowds to gather I realized. Again, this was purposely done—if you have loose machines and more winners, you want others to be able to vicariously enjoy it. That stimulates them to recharge their batteries and play more. I'm beginning to truly appreciate the role that psychology plays in the decision of where to place the slots. Great care has evidently been taken in placing these machines just so.

The slot machines surrounding the table-game area were also getting relatively heavy play and the aisles were fairly full. But I did notice that the end machines were not getting as much play as the machines in the middle and at the end farthest away from the tables.

I think the slot players prefer not to be near the table-game players and vice versa. Watched as many table players put some coins in the end machines as they wandered away from games. A few won. They pocketed their winnings. None bothered to sit down.

This is too good to be true. The machines and how they're played are fitting the profiles given by Mr. Handle almost to a "T." If I were to watch for a year straight, would every day be like this one? Or have I just hit one of those days where everything is working out according to theory?

Now to the crosswalks and to the visible machines. They are getting heavy play. The slot aisles are crowded and although there is some spreading out—player, empty machine, player, empty machine—there are quite a few aisles where players are sitting next to each other. Is the crowd the reason the visible machines in the crosswalks are getting played—again, just as Mr. Handle said? Are some people moved (unconsciously) to seek a little leg room, and does this bring them unwittingly (and fortuitously) to the loose machines? Mr. Handle and his crowd of slot managers and programmers are geniuses to have designed such a system.

*Boom! Just left the lounge after writing the above and we've got a BIG winner not far from the change booth! Big crowd gathering around her or is it a him? Two people were jumping up and down and screaming and hugging. I assume they know each other. BIG CROWD gathers. Wow! People are almost giddy. No, people **are** giddy. I think I actually see looks of ecstasy on the faces of the winners' fellow slot players. This is the DREAM. Every slot player is putting him or herself in the position of the winners. I can't really get close to the machine to see what was won but it's a dollar machine—a loose dollar machine—and it hit for the maximum. (I checked it out later— it was $10,000. And it was a progressive machine, not one of the better bets in the slot machine gamble.)*

*And it is exciting. I've been in casinos before when BIG jackpots are hit. Mr. Handle couldn't have planned it better. I keep wondering if it's like this every day—are the profiles so perfect? Where are the fluctuations for short term play? Or are there just so many machines that the fluctuations are smoothed over (mostly) even on a single day? So the loose machines **as a whole** conform to their looseness profile? And the tight machines **as a whole** reflect their tight profile? Individual machines may fluctuate wildly but a group of machines evens everything out. That coffee-shop area seems to have the happiest players in the casino—it also seems to have quite a few regulars, even tonight. My basic question as I saunter around is whether you play here a lot.*

Quite a few people are waiting in line at the change booth, I noticed.

Later on in the evening some screams come from the crosswalk across the casino from me. Another winner? I rush over and someone has hit a $1,200 payout. A small crowd was gathering even as I arrived.

The aisles are filled with players and I'd estimate that 50 to 60 percent of the machines are being played. No wonder this place makes a fortune from these machines.

At midnight, I realize that I've been watching for three hours. Went so fast. Casino is still going but you can see that many people have left. Time for me to go too.

Have I learned what I think I've learned?

Saturday: 11 AM to 1 PM

Right away I can notice a difference. There's a big crowd here at this time, much bigger than at a comparable time on Wednesday. The weekends really bring out the people.

*Went to the coffee shop first. Place is packed. All week-enders—except for one lady who had been here on Wednesday ("I come four days a week and I always play this machine. This is **my** machine!")—but many said that they come once a month, once every two months—quite a few indicated that these machines were the only ones they played. A few individuals said they put in eight to ten hours on the machines when they do come! Of course, there was the usual assortment of people who had no idea as to why they had selected the particular machine that they were playing on.*

Every several seconds, it seems, you hear coins hitting trays. It sounds like all anyone ever does is win, win, win at the slots. Of course, you only need one machine going off here and there, there and here, to create the illusion that there are winners, winners everywhere.

I am gaining a deep appreciation for the intelligence behind the slot machines. Smart machines, smart programmers, and brilliant placement decisions made by casino executives such as Mr. Handle.

At the table-game area, the tables have quite a bit of action. The end machines even have a few people on them. I watch for 10 minutes and every single person who was playing those end machines has left . . . they've gone either deeper into their row or to another slot aisle farther in. After another 10 minutes, I witness what I've witnessed time and again . . . a table-game player strolls over and puts some coins in. He loses them and moves on.

There's a scream somewhere in the slot area. Another big winner. I'm beginning to realize that many slot players love to scream. Based on the screams you can't tell if someone has won a million dollars, ten thousand dollars, a thousand dollars or several hundred dollars. But those screams certainly pump the adrenaline into you.

Now here's something to think about: I've been in casinos for years and years playing the table games, and I only vaguely remember the sheer volume of noise, human and machine, that formed the background against which I played. Now that I'm focusing on the slot machines and the slot areas, I am acutely aware of the level of noise—the clanging coins, the shouts of joy. And I actually do feel the adrenaline rushing in me and, strangely, in all the people around me.

Strange dichotomy—that for many, playing the slots is a relaxing activity and simultaneously an energizing one. You can relax and get psyched at the same time. I never would have thought the machines would have this emotional underpinning. Indeed, I've never really heard anyone extol the excitement to be found in the slot areas. And there is, there is. This has to be another reason for playing them. The anticipatory delight is palpable.

The visible machines are also getting heavy play and the aisles are relatively crowded. I ask some of the people at the visible machines what caused them to select these. Most had no idea, some said they wanted more room, others that these were their favorite machines and they always played here.

I am going to start testing my theory—my selection principle theory—I just got a revelation, I'll call it my Darwinian Slot Selection Principle—right now.

I journey into the rows upon rows of slot machines. Here's what I'm looking for. Are the people playing the loose machines and those mid-range machines regular patrons of the casino? Are they **as a group** more conscious of why they are selecting the machines they are playing on? Have they been unconsciously guided to these particular machines because of their higher payouts? Wait a minute. All this is too complicated. I just need a simple formula—do the better-paying machines tend to attract the regulars over time? That's it. Are regular players, be it consciously or unconsciously, drawn to the better-paying machines through a process of elimination or natural selection? That's it. The regular players are being *"self-selected" through trial and error to play the better machines.*

So, if I go into the regular aisles, I should find more people who aren't regulars, who only come a few times a year or who play at many casinos or something like that.

Of course, Saturday might not be the best day to work this out. But I am getting the distinct impression that the coffee-shop crowd, for example, has through trial and error found their way to those machines.

So I plunged into the slot aisles and asked people how often they came, and how they selected their machines. I got what I was looking for. Some said they were regulars, came once or twice a week or several times a month. Most came intermittently. But here's what I'm noticing. The degree of awareness is decidedly less in the aisles than on the visible machines or in the coffee-shop area. Only a handful of the hundreds of people I'm casually talking to in the slot aisles have any idea as to why they play the machine they are playing. The reverse is true of the other areas. Quite a few people, as I've already noted, have told me they play a particular machine or in a particular area because they win more or have had more luck in these areas.

This is my Darwinian Selection Principle in action! I wish I could find out exactly where the loose machines are in all the casinos in America and really see if this selection principle works universally. Are regular players drawn to the better machines over time? I would say yes!

I check the time—brother! it's 2:30.

I decide I'll go right through until six o'clock, then take a nap, have dinner and hit the casino later that night for my final round of observations. But first I'll go to the coffee shop and get something for lunch.

Saturday Afternoon Continued

Lunch was interesting. I had to wait in a long line and as I did I was able to watch the slot players in the coffee-shop area. These machines do hit quite frequently—a lot of low and medium payouts. The players, many of whom were here this morning, are loyal to their machines. There isn't as much of a player turnover as in the table-game area or even, if superficial observations mean anything, in the slot aisles. Some slot players waiting in line with me would run over and spell other slot players who would take their place in line. They didn't want to give up their machines. A group of five ladies did this for the 20 minutes I was waiting on line. Four were playing and one would hold the place in line. Then one would leave and take the lady's place on line and so forth. And this was the comp line! We all had comps for lunch but the place was so crowded that we had to wait 20 minutes to get seated. Amazing.

At lunch I just listened. I'm actually writing this at lunch. Sure enough, the sounds of slot play swirl around the coffee shop. I'm sure most people aren't consciously listening as I am, but I'm also sure that for slot players the unconscious is processing the noise of coins hitting trays and the occasional squeal of delight. The unconscious minds of the slot players are hearing what they want to hear and, by doing so, the slot players are programming themselves with the desire to play more. Or am I beginning to psychobabble? Makes sense, though. I'm an hour at lunch writing down most of today's observations.

The casinos want the players to rush out after lunch and grab the first machine that they see—and what's great from the casino perspective is that most of the machines that the lunch crowd will select will not be near the coffee shop because these machines are already packed. So the players will naturally go to the aisles where there are more tight machines waiting to ambush them! So what will my job be? To focus the player's desire in the right direction. Lead them to the best machines possible. The casino instills in the player an ever-expanding desire to play and I give the player the tools to select the best opportunity for victory. Dramatic, but that's really what a gambling writer does.

By four o'clock I'm back wandering around the casino. There's heavy action all over. There are tiny ebbs and flows that I notice. Some slot aisles are jammed, others are only half full. When I left the coffee shop, the crowd was small inside but the machines outside were full.

The table-game area is getting the most action I've seen thus far with maybe half the machines being played. Maybe a third of the end ones are being played. I feel kind of bad for the people playing those end machines, knowing as I do that they are returning a mere 83 percent. I do notice in a half hour of watching that people are moving from these machines rather frequently; this seems to be a pattern for these end machines in the table area. But they are getting more play than I've ever seen. Of course, the table games themselves are crowded.

In the slot aisles, I can see that the visible machines are getting good action. These people I'm happy for because they are getting the best slot machine paybacks the casino has to offer. This is funny—funny ironic, not funny ha! ha!—I'm beginning to let my emotions out. I am now deciding who I'm happy for and who I'm sad for.

I start to ask my questions of the players: Why did you select this machine? How often do you play? and so on. The pattern of the answers seems unwavering. Most, in fact the overwhelming majority, of the people in the slot aisles, have no idea why they selected the machines they are playing on. They just picked a machine at random. I'm getting this response much more frequently than I had previously. Are the Saturday afternoon players less insightful than the morning players?

My guess is that the mid-week players, the weekend and mid-week regulars, and those who actually study the machines (or are cognizant of their bankrolls) are more alert. When I go to the coffee-shop area, the visible machines and the change-booth area, I am getting more variation in my answers:

"This is my lucky machine."

"I want more room."

"The aisles are too crowded."

"I was losing over there and the guy who was here had won, so I moved."

"I always play these machines."

"Best machines in the house."

These comments, or some such like them, were not unusual. It's given me another idea to go along with my Darwinian Slot Selection Principle—*actually it's an idea I'm lifting from another writer on another topic but I think it might just be the way to capitalize on the Darwinian principle. . . .*

I'm tired. It's 6:30. Time flies when you're theorizing!

Saturday: 10 PM to 1 AM

Did I really expect anything different?

The casino is packed to overflowing and the slot aisles are filled to near-capacity. There are people actually waiting to play the machines by the coffee shop and every single visible machine has players on them. The change-booth machines are also jammed and long lines are everywhere. The sounds of coins hitting trays fill the slot areas. It all sounds like thunderclaps from the gods of chance.

But there is something different about this night.

If I said there was palpable excitement in the afternoon, tonight it's heart-thumping time. Here comes another foreign thought—I say "foreign" because I don't usually think like this but . . . is there a synergistic, subliminal chemical or psychic or combination of chemical-psychical reaction taking place in the slot areas?

Are people emanating such powerful desires, the equivalent of gambling pheromones (to win, to be rich, to have money, to cojoin with Lady Luck), that the sheer numbers of people so desiring increase the individual's desire in a geometric way, with this in turn creating one huge gestalt desire that all slot players dip into? A renewing, overwhelming slot-player stream of collective unconscious that pushes its individual members to play, play, play those machines and swim in the river of chance? Wow! A Jungian psychological collective unconscious, perhaps fueled by the chemistry of anticipation?

I feel it.

I look around at all these people pumping in coins and pulling handles and pressing buttons and the constant clanging of coins hitting trays, the occasional screams or squeals, and, oh boy, people are engaged in some tribal yet highly individualistic totemic something-or-other with the slot machine itself the very totem and simultaneously the god and object of their veneration. I can't find other words for it.

Are the players tonight all caught up in some primal drive connected to a computer-driven entity? Is this worship that I'm watching? I feel it and I'm not even playing—and, strangely, I don't even have a desire to play. There is a god in the machine after all, a god that chooses who shall win and who shall lose—

*a blind watcher that selects which coinal sacrifices will be re-
warded and which will be rejected. Cain and Abel on a slot
machine? Would a person at a losing machine watching a
winner want to kill that person?*

It's exciting! It's exciting!

*I'm walking around this casino with my eyes open. I'm not
playing. I'm watching as I've never watched before. My consciousness has taken a quantum leap as a watcher because
some other sense is kicking in. There is ecstasy in the slot
aisles. Ecstasy and pain and torment and desire and . . . madness! I'm looking at the faces of some of the players and there's
a divine madness in their eyes.*

*Mid-week and the afternoons had nothing even approaching
this. Saturday night is worship time! No wonder people stay at
the tight machines! This gestalt of man, machine, desire and
programming has created a consciousness that pervades the
slot aisles and is reflected in so many happily possessed faces.*

*I've seen this before at craps games when a shooter is on a
torrid roll, but I never witnessed it in quite this way. At slots
it's hundreds of individuals, playing at individual machines,
sharing a gestalt psyche! A craps game is more communal—
people are rooting together on a hot shooter, their money riding
in his hot, dice-throwing hands. But the slot player is an individual human unit playing an individual machine unit. Yet
I sense there is a bond, albeit unconscious, but very real nevertheless, that is uniting the slot players in a great whirling der-
vish of hope, anticipation and angst.*

*This would explain why people play—perhaps it's the final
piece in the puzzle as to why people would play at machines
that everyone knows you can't beat! Like bees in a hive, the
players buzz about the slot machines feeding their Queens—
the machines. They share a singular consciousness; the slot
area on a Saturday night is a giant hive, a gestalt entity, with
one mission: to feed the Queen.*

I didn't even interview people tonight.

I didn't want to interfere with their worship.

*Besides, isn't just about everything Mr. Handle told me con-
firmed by my own observations? I think so. But does he know
what is released on these Saturday evenings in his casinos?
Does he appreciate the songs of the machines, the clinging,*

clanging and juke-box music sounds—the metal mantras—that put the slot players into altered states of consciousness? My guess is that he and all the other casino executives know exactly what they are doing and what effects their decisions have on the players. If I carry the beehive analogy one step further, then Mr. Handle and all the Mr. Handles of the casino world are beekeepers and the casinos are their hives.

Well, maybe I can throw some clever bees into their mix—some bees that can produce more honey for themselves and less for the beekeepers.

8

The Darwinian Slot Selection Principle

I am writing now in the calm light of dawn.

It has been months since I wrote the above reflections on my observations of Mr. Handle's casino(s). Since that occasion I have visited his casino(s) several more times, plus I've observed slot players in casinos in Atlantic City, Mississippi and Nevada. Indeed, some nights the slot areas fairly hum like a hive and that dramatic sense of altered consciousness that I felt after many hours of observation that particular Saturday still inspires me to think that something quite profound happens to many slot players on certain nights in the casinos. Could it be a mix of player fatigue and hope, coupled with the sounds of the slots—the bells, the little musical ditties, the coins hitting trays—plus those reels spinning, the colored lights flashing, and, perhaps, a chemical released in all those excited people (a slot "pheromone"?) that causes one's psyche to suddenly go into overdrive? Is it this ecstatic sense that keeps bringing some inveterate slot players back to the casinos time after time, win or lose?

I think a neurochemical analysis of long-time slot players might show that changes have taken place in their brains and that these changes are quite similar to the neurochemical changes that take place in people during transcendental or mystical experiences. Certainly, that would explain the ecstatic looks on the faces of so many slot players.

Of course, what about all those *angry* (losing) faces? Not everyone in a slot area, even on a humming Saturday night, is chanting the mechanical one-armed bandit version of *Hare Krishna*.

So I guess everyone can't be a mystic.

But I have learned something else from my observations, however, something a little more practical and far more useful to slot players looking to get an edge.

From my observations it seems pretty clear that "regulars"—defined as people who play a given casino one, two, three or more times a week—tend to play at looser machines. They don't know *a priori* which slots are looser, but through a selection principle every bit as real as Darwin's survival of the fittest, regular slot players must ultimately find the loose machines or die, economically speaking. It's an evolutionary system that requires the player to adapt so that he plays to a more hospitable environment (defined as the looser machines) or face the very real possibility of going economically extinct.

From my interviews with regulars playing at the loose machines in Mr. Handle's casino(s), it was fairly obvious from their comments that these players felt they had had "good luck" at these machines and so had stayed. The overwhelming majority of the regulars had found "their" machines through trial and error but, once found, stuck with them. This would explain why so many of the visible machines, those machines in the crosswalks and small or elevated carousels, were being played rather heavily in the weekday mornings and afternoons by regulars.

The *Darwinian Slot Selection Principle* is quite logical once grasped. In fact, it's so obvious and self-evident that for the life of me I can't figure out why anyone hasn't written about this before, or even thought of it. *Regulars will more than likely be playing the loosest machines in the casinos.* That's why they *are* regulars—the casino has been relatively lucky for them. Otherwise they would have sought out other venues for their slot play.

So how does this *Darwinian Slot Selection Principle* work? Let's take a step-by-step, albeit simplistic, example of how someone who played frequently at a given casino would be moved to "discover" the loose slots there—and thus become a "regular."

The Story of Marty Darwin

Trip One

Marty Darwin comes to the casino this afternoon. It's his first time in this particular casino. He goes to the slot machines by the table-game pit. He plays for an hour, loses, goes to have something to eat, then comes back to these very same machines. He plays for another hour and loses some more. That's it for that particular bank of machines. Now he walks to another bank, still in the table-game area. He spends two more hours, at the end of which time he has lost his stake for that day. He goes home disappointed and upset.

Trip Two

Marty comes back to the casino and goes over to the machines deep in the slot area, as far away from the table-game pits as he can get. He feels that those machines "over there" aren't lucky for him and he's hoping to have a better day at these machines. If not, he won't be coming back to this casino in the near future.

And he does have a much better day than last time. He wins a few dollars before lunch. After lunch, he comes right back to the machine that he had been playing. Thankfully, no one is there. He plays for three hours and loses. But he has made a profit for the day. He goes home happy and intends to return here again.

Trip Three

Marty thinks of this as his lucky day. He heads straight for the same machine that he had played last time. Unfortunately, Wilma is at that machine. Wilma notices that Marty's face dropped when he found her playing the machine.

"Forget it," she says. "You want this machine, you can have it! I've been losing on it all day!"

Wilma gets up and goes to another slot bank. Marty can't wait to get on his machine. If it's been cold all day, it's bound to be hot when he plays it.

Two hours later, Marty is unhappy. While he hasn't been clobbered, he has lost a considerable amount. He toys with the idea of moving to another machine. Finally, after another half hour spent chasing his losses, Marty reluctantly gives up his machine. He's down but not out.

He goes to lunch.

There's a small line at the coffee shop, so he watches the men and women playing the machines nearby. He's excited to hear the coins hitting the trays. During lunch those same sounds can be heard inside the coffee shop and they form a background noise that Marty is only dimly aware of. Still, Marty can't wait to finish his lunch so he can get back into the action. After lunch, Marty decides to play on a machine outside the coffee shop. He doesn't really know why he has made that decision.

After two hours, he's up a small amount on this particular machine and he is quite content to go home with his small win. The day has otherwise been a washout. However, it ended well and he plans to return.

Trip Four

Marty Darwin returns, his money in hand, and he is ready for the slot wars. He decides to head for the machines by the coffee shop. When he had been playing there on his last visit, he overheard some of his fellow players saying that they had been very lucky on these machines. His unconscious mind has retained this information, although Marty himself has "forgotten" it.

After four hours of continuous play, Marty is up a small amount. This is his second win on these machines in a row. He decides to skip lunch and take his win home.

Trip Five

This time Marty loses on his favorite machine—and it's his own fault. After two hours of play, he was up a considerable amount—then he got greedy and put it all back. His loss is small. Next time Marty vows to take the money and run. Oh, he'll be coming back all right.

Trip Six

Same machine. This time Marty took the money and ran. After an hour of play, he hit a relatively big jackpot. Instead of putting it all back, Marty cashed in his coins and went home. He didn't even bother with lunch.

Trip Seven

Same machine. Marty loses but not a lot. He played for three hours, had a good time, no harm done. He also likes the people in the coffee-shop area. He's actually making some friends. He got a comp for lunch.

Trip Eight

Marty goes right to his machine and sure enough, someone else is on it. This particular gentleman isn't like Wilma—he doesn't care that Marty gives a hurt look. "This machine is hotter than hell," says the gentleman to Marty. Marty decides to go to another machine by the coffee shop. He breaks even for the day. But all the time he was playing, he kept watching the man at "his" machine. The man was still there when Marty decided to call it a day so Marty never discovered that the man had lost everything he had previously won and then some.

Trip Nine

Hurrah! Marty's machine is not taken! He sits and starts playing and has a fairly lucky day. He also has a comped lunch. This is a good trip and he's meeting quite a few people who play in "his" area, as he's come to think of the coffee-shop machines.

Future Trips

Marty has now become a "regular." Trip after trip he has decent luck on these machines by the coffee shop. He isn't up. In fact, overall he's losing. But he has won enough times that those good feelings have lingered and colored his perception of these particular machines. His other friends, not his "coffee-shop friends," have all lost much more than him in that same period of time at other casinos. And they bet about what he does. He keeps telling them to try "his" casino but they're stubborn. Marty is now quite friendly with several other regulars and all these regulars agree on one thing—these machines by the coffee shop are good! Then one day a writer named Frank Scoblete approaches Marty Darwin. This writer is a good-looking, sexy . . . (Okay, okay, I'm getting carried away.) This writer asks Marty why he plays this particular machine and Marty replies, "I've been lucky here." And the writer wonders if many regulars don't eventually wind up playing the better-paying machines just through an evolutionary selection principle that he has yet to name.

Now, in the real world, chances are the *Darwinian Slot Selection Principle* operates in a more subtle and more compli-cated way than in my little story above. However, I do be-lieve, based upon my observations in Mr. Handle's casino(s), that the regular players are likely to have found the truly loose machines in the casinos they frequent. Whether they are fully aware of this fact is irrelevant. They can chalk it up to luck, to their good living, to their rabbit's foot, to whatever they want; but in actuality, by trial and error, they have hit upon the better-paying machines because the accumulation of their play throughout the casino has *guided* them to these machines. The tight machines were not conducive to eco-nomic survival; the loose machines were. A simple and ele-gant evolutionary principle.

The next step is to capitalize on this observation.

The Julian Method of Slot Selection

In the book *The Julian Strategies in Roulette* (Paone Press), author John F. Julian outlines a unique method for selecting potentially biased roulette wheels without having to do the thousands upon thousands of observations necessary to "clock" a wheel. He calls it "looking for the lucky lady or the fortunate fella."

Great ideas are always simple and Mr. Julian's idea is no exception. Simply look for someone who is winning big at a roulette wheel and bet with her or him because she or he is the "lucky lady or fortunate fella." Why do this? Because it is quite possible that the "lucky lady or fortunate fella" is a wheel clocker who has found a biased wheel, or, somewhat rarer, the individual is a "wheel tracker;" that is, someone who can anticipate with great accuracy where the ball will land. Now, if you have actually found a "wheel clocker" or a "wheel tracker," your odds of beating roulette increase immensely. If you haven't, well, says Julian, no harm done—the odds haven't increased against you by betting with a lucky individual. That's his notion and it's a good one.

Now, since imitation is the sincerest form of flattery, Mr. Julian will be flattered no end by the fact that I'm borrowing his idea and using it for slots.

Want a good method for finding the loosest slots in a given casino without having to clock a machine for months to figure out what it's returning or without having your own Mr. Handle tell you exactly where he has placed the loose machines? Find some regulars who swear by a certain area and play there! It might take a little work. You might have to walk around a bit and talk to some people. You'll have to ask how often a person comes here to play and other such questions, but in the long run, if I'm right in assuming from my personal observations at Mr. Handle's casino(s) that the regulars invariably find the loosest slots, you will be better off. And if I'm wrong—as Mr. Julian asserts—no harm done. You haven't decreased your chances of winning.

Coupled with what Mr. Handle has already revealed about slot placement, the Julian Method of Slot Selection—or "finding the lucky regular"—might go a long way towards your breaking the one-armed bandits!

9

Expert Strategies

Breaking the One-Armed Bandits,
Tournament Play and Comps

You now know the most important information ever revealed about the slot machines—where they are located in a given casino and the thinking behind this placement. With Mr. Handle's information, intelligently applied and adapted to the particular casinos where you play, you have a great chance of selecting the loose machines. If you couple this with a little research of your own—using the Julian Method of Slot Selection—you can be fairly confident that you have the best machine-selection principles ever discovered.

So the first and most important step in successful slot play was to locate your machine. You have THE METHOD for doing this.

The next step is to actually play it.

There are many methods for doing that.

In the process of researching and writing this book, I personally interviewed hundreds of slot players and my researchers interviewed many hundreds more. Sadly, most slot players did not have any particular game plan for beating the machines. In fact, most just brought a certain amount of money to the casino and, when they lost that, their playing for that day was at an end. My single greatest finding in an otherwise disappointing survey of 2,000 slot players was that the majority played until they lost all their money! The few who actually went home winners did so because they had won rather large jackpots that they *couldn't lose* before leaving the casino for the day!

Also in the process of researching and writing this book, I spoke to other gaming authorities who not only play the slots but write about them as well. Some of their advice was invaluable for the structuring and writing of this book.

One of the best slot players/writers is Jim Hildebrand, whose slot reports appear regularly in *The Casino Player* magazine. Not only is Mr. Hildebrand a fine writer, but his slot-playing advice is based on years of savvy and, as he calls it, "playing to win for fun!" We have already heard from Mr. Handle, a brilliant casino executive, and I thought it only proper to give a brilliant long-time player's perspective to go along with that.

Jim Hildebrand writes about and plays slots as an "enjoyable diversion" from his regular and "stressful" career of the running a large corporate enterprise.

Frank: So why do you personally play the slots?

Mr. Hildebrand: I deal with people all day—labor unions, lawyers, bankers, some of which is adversarial—and playing the slots for me is a healthy diversion. I really enjoy a people-oriented profession, but some time away from people—just you and a machine—is a great change of pace. I find playing a slot or video-poker machine to be totally relaxing, almost meditative. I do play table games frequently, but I've been known to win at blackjack and then head straight for the machines. Often at a table game people can get confrontational, and I have enough of that in real life. So while I often find the other players at table games interesting, it is not as relaxing. I find my time at a slot machine or video-poker machine to be more peaceful.

Frank: Do you think this could be another explanation as to why so many people play the machines—in addition to the chance to win big money?

Mr. Hildebrand: Absolutely. I also think that table games require work. If you are going to be an expert blackjack player or craps player, you have a lot of work to do to get to that level of play. I think that slot players as a whole are truly recreational gamblers. They are playing for fun. For the most part, they are playing for small stakes. Keep in mind that most people work very hard at *real* work, so why would they want to work hard at *reel* work? I think this is a contributing factor in the explosive growth of the slot machines. It's fun and it could be profitable.

Frank: But you have serious methods of play. You have a game plan. You know what machines you're going to play and how you're going to play them. You don't just sit at the first machine you see. Even if you are a recreational player, a fun player, you are also an expert player insofar as experience, technique and reflection can make one an expert player at the slots. There are better and worse slot players and you're one of the best. So your ideas and insights are valuable.

Mr. Hildebrand: Where do you want to begin?

Frank: Although I have a placement scheme by a casino executive in my book, I still want to know how you, personally, pick the machines you're going to play.

Mr. Hildebrand: Well, I'll tell you what I *don't* do first. I don't play any of the giant progressive jackpot machines—those are absolutely out. The odds are astronomical to begin with and in order to get the money for the big jackpot, the casinos have to skimp on the medium payouts. So to have a shot at the big one, you are giving up a good return on the medium-size payouts. Except for the lucky individuals who hit a giant progressive jackpot, and those don't occur very often, these machines are really not worth playing for the long-term. So if you intend to play slots for any length of time or enjoy the recreational aspects of slot play, you should stay away from these machines. They'll drain you dry much quicker than other machines.

I recommend the non-progressive machines with the good intermediate payouts of 200, 300 and 400 coins. I never attempt to play for the big jackpot on any machine I select because the odds are too high and it's too easy to get caught up in a jackpot mania and lose track of your bankroll. Big jackpots are actually a distraction, so I set my sights on the intermediate payouts, which will occur more often on any machine. If you get your share of these, you can walk away a winner.

Frank: So your first rule of thumb is not to play for the primary jackpot, even on non-progressive machines.

Mr. Hildebrand: Right. Secondly, I always play full coin, because I play short sessions and I'm always looking for what I call "short-term leverage," which is the maximum multiple on that pay table. Before I walk in a casino, I have a session plan in mind. If I'm going to Vegas, I will map out which casinos and which machines I'm playing based on previous trips. I always scout out machines. I don't just pick a machine at random. I invest serious effort to empirically identify the best-paying machines.

Frank: Explain what you mean by "scouting."

Mr. Hildebrand: During my trips, I make notes concerning what machines in which casinos I've had success on or others have had success on. Because even the best-paying machines have cold streaks (and vice versa), the data should be collected continuously over several trips. I write down exactly where these machines are located. I'll even write down the serial numbers of the machines so that should the casino move them, as sometimes occurs, I can walk around and find them at their new locations. I have a list of machines that I'm planning to play on every trip I take.

Frank: You think that previous success might be an indicator of a looser machine?

Mr. Hildebrand: Certainly it's one of the criteria, especially on the medium range of payouts. If you find that you have consistent success with a given machine in this payout range, then it makes sense to find and try that machine on subsequent visits. How long you play that machine depends upon the trend of the machine at that time. Keeping records is only common sense. So I have my game plan formulated beforehand. I give myself so much time on previously scouted machines but I also allow a certain amount of time for random play and additional scouting. You want to be flexible within the confines of your overall game plan. But remember, playing slots should be fun, so your plan should not be rigid.

Frank: How would you structure a day, say, in Las Vegas?

Mr. Hildebrand: Well, Las Vegas is the best place to play slots in the United States because the competition among the casinos allows for much looser machines overall than you would find anywhere else in the country. And downtown Las Vegas has the loosest slots of all. For a day in Las Vegas, I would plan separate playing sessions where I might hit several different casinos during each session. So in the morning, I would take one part of my daily stake and divide that roughly into the number of casinos I planned to visit. Some casinos might be allocated more stake than others. So now I have several mini-stakes with which to play a single morning session. I might start the morning session at Caesars, play for a while there; move across the street to the Flamingo Hilton, play there; then go to Harrah's and finish there. So my morning session might consist of three mini-sessions at three different casinos. In the afternoon, I would go downtown and quite possibly I'd hit downtown in the evening too. The majority of my play, overall, would be where I am staying and being comped, usually Caesars or The Golden Nugget.

You could always do a full session at one casino, of course, but I enjoy going from casino to casino. I should reiterate that I play slots to win but also for fun—I have no illusions about the fact that I am facing a negative expectation. I approach the game intelligently and I try to get the best game I can get. I don't want to hand over my money without a struggle and I play hard to win, but when all is said and done, I play for fun. I think what I try to do in my writing about slots is also get across the idea of winning, which is really the fun aspect of playing. So going from casino to casino is a part of the fun I have in playing the machines. It's also a way to break up a losing trend. If things aren't going right at one of the mini-sessions, you know that you can just pick yourself up and go across the street for a new session. You have a built-in break. The anticipation of a fresh start is invigorating.

Frank: So on a trip to Vegas you have a total bankroll and you break it up into daily stakes, session stakes, and mini-session stakes?

Mr. Hildebrand: I divide the total bankroll into the number of days I'm staying, then divide the daily bankroll into sessions and then casino mini-sessions. The number of sessions is not important but the reasoning behind it is. You should never allow yourself to lose more than one mini-session's amount at a time. You want a natural check on losses, and mini-session stakes are a way to do that.

Frank: How do you decide when a session or a mini-session is over?

Mr. Hildebrand: Obviously, if you lose a mini-session's bank-roll, you would move on. However, I also move on if I've hit my "quit point."

Frank: Explain your concept of "quit point."

Mr. Hildebrand: In advance, on certain machines, I will select a hit frequency that I should expect. I call this my "expected frequency" system of play. The overall objective is to finish that machine with more coins than you started with. I play a certain number of pulls based on the expected hit frequency. If the machine is in a good trend, hitting more frequently, I'll keep playing, building coins beyond the original stake. Once the trend falls off, *below the expected*, I hit the "quit point" and pick up and move— but I'm still ahead for that machine. If, on the other hand, the machine is in a bad trend and doesn't hit its expected frequency in short order, that's the downside "quit point" and I'm out of there quickly.

The key to this method of playing is knowing the expected frequency of each type of machine and having those quit points firmly in your mind. To just play with abandon and hope is a disastrous trap.

Now, if I'm winning consistently on the machine, I set aside a certain portion of my wins—I won't touch those. So with each payout, I will put aside a given percentage. I won't touch that no matter what. I keep ratcheting up the quit point (my Ratchet Theory) to protect my winnings. Once the trend falls off to that quit point, I will leave the machine. That mini-session is over. In this way, I can still walk away with some coins in my pocket and probably even a win.

Frank: Many of the slot players I've interviewed, in fact, the overwhelming majority, don't have a money management scheme such as that. They just play until they lose everything they brought with them.

Mr. Hildebrand: Frank, watching that happen to people, over and over, is the reason I started writing about slot play. You're right, the ability, or rather the discipline, to stop playing is absolutely the toughest thing for slot players—and the most important. Taking money and running is hard to do. But if you want any chance of winning, you have to have a money management plan, a way of getting up with a win in your pocket, instead of a win given back to the machine. Taking a percentage from each payout is a good way to do that. You have to recognize that your playing time may be less, because you are not playing back those wins and playing right back into the casino's "recycle scheme."

Frank: What other playing scheme would you recommend?

Mr. Hildebrand: There's a type of play I call the "Bully Method." It is a little more dangerous than the "expectation" style of play, but for more aggressive players, it is a fun attack on the machine. First, you find the machine you know to have a high payout and then select a mid-range jackpot and then "bully" the machine until you hit it—or lose your mini-session stake! It's an all-or-nothing style of play where you feed back all your winnings in the machine in an attempt to get that jackpot. The jackpot must be a mid-range one that has a decent expected frequency.

Let us say that I'm looking to hit the 240-coin payout on a certain machine—which is not an outrageous goal. That's my objective for that session—one hit of 240. As soon as I hit that 240-coin payout, I take the coins and run! I can invest up to a limit of, say, 180 coins, and if the machine hits the 240 before I lose my limit, I get a great win, but *only* if I take the 240 and go! In video poker, I shoot for a certain level hand before my quit point: quads in Jacks-or-Better, or a straight flush in Double Jokers.

Frank: Do you recommend playing in slot tournaments?

Mr. Hildebrand: Well, there are good slot tournaments and there are "not as good" slot tournaments. A good one returns all the entrance fees in the form of prizes. A "not as good" one doesn't, and they are the vast majority. However, these are still a good play if the hold is less than 10 percent. Playing in a good slot tournament is one of the best deals you can get in a casino.

Frank: Explain how you know which is which.

Mr. Hildebrand: Sometimes the casinos make it easy for you because they advertise it that way—"All entrance fees are returned in the form of prizes!" If not, you simply multiply the number of entrants by the fee and then divide the amount of the prizes into the total. If you come up with zero, they are paying back all the money in the form of prizes. In such a tournament the casino has no edge over you whatsoever. Think of a prize-pool top prize of say, $40,000, and 250 entrants. Where are you going to find a bet that gives you a one in 250 shot at winning that kind of money—with no vig taken out by the casino? So a full payback tournament is great—it's the best deal you can get as a slot player.

Frank: But if you multiply the number of entrants by the fee and divide the prizes and you come up with less than zero, it's not a good tournament?

Mr. Hildebrand: Unless you are getting some comps that make up the difference. If the tournament is giving you a free room, free meals and so on, you have to estimate what that is worth and figure it into what the casino is holding back per tournament player. You might find that the comps and the prizes actually wind up coming to a greater-than-zero amount so that you are actually involved in a positive expectation.

Frank: What are the various formats for the tournaments that you play?

Mr. Hildebrand: Most slot tournaments are speed tournaments where you have a time limit to generate as many points as possible. A more enjoyable one is where you are given a certain number of credits on your machine and you have a certain amount of time to play them and to generate maximum points.

Frank: Any recommendations for playing these?

Mr. Hildebrand: The single most important thing for tournament slots is to pick the right tournaments to play in. That's the overriding concern—enter the right tournaments, the ones that give you the most in comps and prizes in relation to your entrance fee. Then play relaxed and, in a speed tournament, hit that button as fast as possible as each payout finishes registering. To pound the button relentlessly is tiring and less effective.

[Apropos of the above discussion, I just received information in the mail concerning a slot tournament being held at the Golden Nugget in Las Vegas. Let's analyze it and see if playing in this tournament would be a good thing for a slot player to do. The entrance fee is $550 and only 150 players will be allowed to play. The prizes are as follows:

1st Place	$25,000
2nd Place	$5,000
3rd Place	$2,500
4th to 50th Place	$550 each
51st to 100th Place	$200 each

Now, the total tournament gross for the Golden Nugget is $82,500 and it's paying out a total of $78,350 in prize money. So the Golden Nugget is netting $4,150, which means that divided over every player, the tournament is costing players an average of $27.66 per player for three nights. However, the players are all being given rooms for three nights, plus a continental breakfast during early-morning rounds, commemorative gifts, and an awards banquet on the third night. Not a bad deal for $27.66.]

The Comping of Slot Players

Frank: How important is it to join slot clubs and receive comps?

Mr. Hildebrand: Very important. The cash-backs and comps take a bit of the sting out of what you may lose at the machines. In addition, it's all a part of the fun of playing—being treated well, getting to know the slot hosts. So I always put my card in the machine and make sure I get full credit for playing. I also put in a certain amount of time at my favorite casinos to make sure that I get full credit. Of course, my favorite casinos have been my luckiest.

Frank: But you don't gear your play towards the attainment of comps?

Mr. Hildebrand: No. Most cash-backs are only .75 to one percent of total play. Rooms and meals kick in another two to five percent. You have to play your game to win. But join the slot clubs at every casino where you play, even if you play there infrequently. You'd be surprised what casinos will offer you to stay at their hotels as opposed to their competition's. When you belong to a slot club, you are given consideration on room prices, meals, shows—quite often you can book a room during peak times when the hotel is booked. You're playing the machines anyway, so you might as well get everything your play is worth.

Hildebrand's Summation

Frank: We've hit on quite a few reasons why someone would play slots. But could you give me some fundamental difference between the stopping of the spinning reels of a machine and, say, the drop of a card in blackjack and the throw of the dice in craps? In all cases we're dealing with luck and the instruments of luck—cards, dice, reels on a machine. Do you see something qualitatively different in slots? Something that we have not yet addressed? Something also that would be another piece in the puzzle that explains the explosive growth of slot play in casinos?

Mr. Hildebrand: I honestly believe that there is a greater mystique about the reels on a slot machine and the workings of a video-poker machine than there is about cards or dice. First, there is just the sheer number of possible ways that the reels can come up. There are so many combinations and so many unknowns that it's almost incalculable by the average brain; you seemingly need a computer to do it. You are dealing with something that is so complex and yet so simple. This alone piques interest. You're playing with a mysterious thing—a slot machine. While purists might disdain reel slots, the truth is that the machine has more mystery surrounding it than other forms of gambling and video poker attracts a certain sophistication and skill. There's almost a mystical thing here. So yes, I see a fundamental qualitative difference between the machines and the table games—with the machines having the edge in mystery.

10

More Expert Strategies

The Matter of Money Management

In craps, blackjack, poker, pai-gow poker, video poker—indeed, in every other casino game—strategies and money management are two entirely different, though equally important, areas of concern. The player has to decide not only what games he'll risk his money on, but what strategies he'll employ when doing so. In blackjack and in all forms of poker, every hand requires a discreet, strategic decision on the part of the player—in addition to how much money to bet.

Not so with the slots. Once you have selected your machine, the only decisions you make are whether to play full coin and when to leave. There are no strategic decisions necessary when the coins are recorded and the reels are spinning. There are no strategic decisions required when the reels stop—except whether you're going to put more coins in the machine or move on.

Thus, money management in slots is the be-all and end-all of play, and all slot playing "systems" or "strategies" are essentially money-management ones. As in anything, there are good and bad money-management schemes. The worst money-management scheme is to play and replay your coins until you go broke, then go out and borrow more and play and play those until you have to rob a bank to recover your losses. You'll meet someone in the next chapter who epitomizes this technique. The best techniques can be boiled down to three types: *Play-Through Techniques, Go-Down Techniques,* and *Percentage-Play Techniques.*

Play-Through Techniques

Let us take a lesson from Jim Hildebrand's playing style. You have "X" amount of money that you have set aside to play the slots for a given trip to your favorite casino. You will divide that money into the number of days that you are staying or playing and get a daily stake. Next, you will divide your daily stake into session stakes by dividing the number of sessions you intend to play in a given day into your daily stake. Essentially this will be our formula for all the techniques I'll recommend.

So now you have your session stake.

Play it through the machine once. *Do not play any of the coins that you win.* You can put those in another bucket, or leave them in the tray, but the cardinal rule here is simple: No coins that come from the machines ever go back in! When you have finished playing your session stake through once, the session is over. You take the coins you've put aside and cash them in. This money is going home with you.

When your next session begins, you do the same. Take your second session stake of the day, play it through once, and pocket the money that comes from the machine. In this way, you are practically guaranteed two things: You will go home with some money in your pocket (if not an actual win) and you will not be wiped out.

Now, to use a single play-through technique, you have to take some things into consideration—the character of your bankroll and the character of . . . well, your character. If you're playing on a short bankroll, you might find that playing through a session stake once doesn't give you enough pulls of the handle to satisfy you. Many players go to a casino for a day and they want to be able to play for four or five hours. Suppose this type of person has only $100 to bet? A hundred dollars can be played through a dollar machine in eight to 12 minutes, a quarter machine in 15 to 20 minutes, if you are playing full coin. For many slot players, such a short stay at the machines is unthinkable.

For someone such as this, the only alternative is to play through a nickel machine at full coin or to play through one quarter at a time in a quarter machine. How would you decide? Check to see if the single quarter has a better payout rate than the full coin on the nickel machines. If so, go with a single quarter. With $100 as your session stake, that gives you 400 pulls of the handle—which for most slot players would translate into a good session of play.

Still, short bankroll or not, the single play-through system requires you to end the session once that session stake has made its way *once* through the bowels of the mechanical beast.

If you are the aggressive type, you might do a double play-through; that is, play your initial session stake through the machine once and then take all the coins that are in the tray (or in a second bucket) and play those through once. This is a rather dangerous approach since you are giving the casino a healthy second whack at your session stake.

Perhaps, an even better way for the aggressive slot player would be to play the initial session stake through once and, if the session has been a winner, take only the winnings (or a percentage of the winnings) and play those through once. After this, win, lose or draw, you would quit that session.

Go-Down Techniques

You have your session stake. Let us say that you have decided to start with five-dollar machines. When you have put half your session stake through the machine, you check the tray, or your second bucket. If the combined amount in the tray and your half-a-session stake is equal to or greater than your total session stake, you will continue to play the next half of your session stake through this denomination machine. However, if it does not add up to the original full-session stake, you will go down to the next level machine—that is, a dollar machine or two-dollar machine (yes, casinos now have this denomination machine).

Now, on this denomination machine, you put through half of your remaining bankroll (that is, one-fourth of the original bankroll). Once this has gone through the machine, you again add what you've won at both the five-dollar machine and at your current machine. If you are ahead (your one-fourth session stake and your winnings exceed your initial session stake), you will return to the five-dollar machine and play through the remaining one-fourth of your session stake at that denomination. However, if you are behind, you will go down to the next level of machine (25 or 50 cents) and play through the remaining one-fourth of your session stake at this level.

The *Go-Down Technique* allows you to stretch your time at the machines without having to exceed a session stake. It also gives you a shot at big money, since your first half-stake will be played at the highest denomination that you can afford.

You could also do a reverse of the *Go-Down Technique* and *go-up* to a higher denomination should you find Lady Luck smiling on you. Let us say that you are having a good session at the one-dollar machines, and you have doubled your session stake at the end of a single play-through. It would not be a bad idea to go to a five-dollar machine and attempt a bigger win. If this appeals to you, take half your winnings and give it a shot. If you lose those winnings, you still leave the session ahead. However, if your luck continues, you could be in for a big payday at this denomination—a far bigger payday than you would have had had you remained at the lower denomination machine.

There is one caveat to this *go-up* concept, a caveat that must be considered even in the original *go-down* technique, and it is this—if you are having good luck at a certain machine, do you really want to leave it? Probably not. I certainly wouldn't abandon a machine that kept paying out.

What to do?

Set a specified number of pulls as your stopping point. Let us say you have won twice your initial session stake at a given machine and you're considering going up to a higher denomination, but you don't want to leave a hot machine. So, don't leave. Give yourself another 10 to 20 pulls on that machine. After this, if you're still increasing your profits, give yourself another 10 to 20 pulls. Keep this up until you reach a point where these pulls finally cost you money. At this point, go up to the next denomination.

Percentage-Play Techniques

You have your session stake. Each decision involves a maximum-specified fixed percentage of your total session stake. Let us say that you are playing with a session stake of $200. You will play *up to* a maximum of five percent per pull. With a $200 session stake, the first pull is for $10. You would go to a five-dollar machine and play two coins. If you should win, you continue playing this machine at $10 a pop until you can go to three coins, $15. You would reach that point when your total session stake plus winnings equaled $300.

Of course, if you lose your first pull at the five-dollar machine, you now have $190. Five percent of that is $9.50. You would play one five-dollar coin, four two-dollar coins, or five one-dollar coins. With each pull you would recalculate what five percent of your total stake is. For this strategy, total stake is the original session stake plus any winnings. You will always play up to five percent of this stake.

The only question you have to ask yourself is, when do you quit a session? A reasonable answer would be to quit a session either when you've lost half your initial session stake or, if you are winning, when you've lost the last 10 pulls in a row.

Underlying Assumptions

There are underlying assumptions in the aforementioned techniques of play. The first is that you look for "loose machines" based upon Mr. Handle's revelations in chapter six and *The Darwinian Slot Selection* and *The Julian Slot Selection Principles* of chapter eight. It's silly to just pick machines at random and then play the above strategies because you aren't giving yourself a chance to get the best bang for your gambling buck. So selecting a good machine is the first and paramount assumption for intelligent slot play.

The second, and just as obvious, assumption is that you play within your comfort zone. Play the denomination of machine that gives you enough time for your risk. If you know that you aren't the type who is satisfied with a quick hit at a high denomination machine, that you need a good several hours of play to feel as if you've given it your "best shot," then pick a "loose machine" in a denomination that you can handle for this amount of time.

Only you can determine what your comfort zone is. But you'll know when you've gone beyond it—you'll start to twitch, fret and sweat.

The third, and final, underlying assumption in all the strategies discussed in this book is their inflexible character. You are going into your slot playing with a predetermined method of attack. You are playing the machine in a machine-like way. Once you have settled upon a strategy that suits you, you must play it perfectly.

To summarize: loose machines + play within comfort zones + perfect execution of strategies selected = a good shot at breaking the one-armed bandits!

Now in the next two chapters, I'd like you to meet two people who represent the extremes of slot play and slot players—the first for ill, the second for good.

11

Poor Grandpa

Any normal person enjoys a dose of weirdness now and again. That's why horror movies are so popular. That's why tales of ghosts rivet us. That's why little kids stare unashamedly at the new and different. Of course, adults just peek and then feel guilty and then tell the little kids to stop staring—it's not polite (peek) to stare.

Me? I'm a connoisseur of the bizarre. I delight in it. In small doses, the weird and wacky can be a wonderful antidote to the average. Feeling pedestrian? Take some medicine for the mundane—enjoy a strange tale.

I've made a kind of hobby of collecting weird bits and pieces of information and some of these concern gambling—strange, or even sobering, tales that I have witnessed myself, or tales witnessed or attested to by good sources that I trust, and other tales that are apocryphal or even made-up. These last *should* be true. Many actually have a moral. Many more don't.

A while ago, a news story made all the major New York media. It was sufficiently strange to merit my attention.

Seems a man was caught robbing a bank.

Now, bank robbery is not so unusual, especially in New York, where bank robbery is the monetary equivalent of take-out. No, what made the story weird were the little details.

The man was 68 years old. He was a grandfather and he had robbed a local bank of $20,000 using his grandson's toy gun.

Why?

Well, when he was first caught, he said it was because of his tremendous medical bills. This was not the whole truth, although the man did have a heart condition for which he was taking pills.

Upon further investigation, the police discovered that Grandpa had robbed the bank to pay off almost $30,000 in gambling debts that he had run up in Atlantic City over the past couple of years—playing the quarter slots.

What's so unusual about that, you say? The psychological literature of gambling is filled with a host of case histories of individuals with gambling fever who ruin their lives—rob, cheat, and sell their possessions and souls—just to get one more dance with Lady Luck. Stupidity is not age-specific. There are plenty of stupid senior citizens in the world. What do you think all those stupid kids you knew when you were growing up grew into—smart adults? Nope—dopes. What's so unusual, then, about a 68-year-old man doing a dumb little bank job?

This.

A couple of years before, Grandpa, on his very first trip to Atlantic City, dropped three—count 'em, three—one, two, three—quarters into a slot machine and . . .

Won $125,000!

He was ecstatic. He bought toys for the grandchildren—even a little gun for his youngest grandson that shot candies into your mouth. Nothing was too good for the family. Grandpa was a hero, a giver of gifts, a man of respect! He loved the attention and devotion paid him by his family, all because he was a man who had harnessed the lightning of luck.

And, of course, he went back to Atlantic City, right away—and then again and again and again and again . . . and again. His chosen casino was more than happy to give this high-rolling, overweight senior citizen a fat credit line that he could draw from.

Now, the ancient Greek philosophers and playwrights knew a thing or two about tragic irony. Here's a piece of it. When you reach the summit, whatever that particular summit may be, you had better be careful because now the lightning bolts of Zeus have a better chance of striking you down. The gods look to bring low those mortals who have dared to rise to the pinnacle. And often the greatest winners suddenly become the most pathetic losers. Just ask Agamemnon. Not only do they fall from the mountaintop—they pratfall off it, slipping on banana peels along the way, only to be met with a custard pie in the face at the bottom. In short, they lose their dignity. We laugh at their suffering.

That was Grandpa. His was a story of a man who lost more than money. He lost his self-esteem.

His game and claim to fame, and later to shame, were the one-armed bandits. In a two-year period, he lost every penny of his $125,000 win (excluding the gifts to the grandchildren); plus he lost all his pension money; plus $30,000 he had taken out in credit from the casino. One pundit, using this story as an example of why gambling is so evil, estimated that grandpa lost $200,000 in two years on those one-armed bandits.

So Grandpa decided to become like them. He would become the human one-armed bandit, and rob a bank and have the tellers put money in *his* belly. He would then take this money to Atlantic City to feed into his more fortunate mechanical brothers who hadn't been fed by his oh-so-gentle hand these past few weeks. Bizarre? Yes. The man would rob a bank to play the slots to pay off the debts that playing the slots had incurred!

Poor Grandpa.

His bad luck in Atlantic City is not what makes this story bizarre, however. His losses had not robbed him of his dignity—after all, they were between him, his wife, and the gods of chance. Nobody else would have to know what a complete idiot he had been. So what if he had stupidly put back everything he had won and then some? The bottom of gambling's Mount Olympus is littered with such losers. Grandpa was in good company. But now he attempted to climb the summit, reach that Olympian height. And, sure enough, that big banana peel was waiting for him at the top.

He planned the robbery perfectly.

He would hit the bank at noon, when the place was packed with patrons. No minimum-wage security guard would chance a gun battle in a crowded noontime bank, Grandpa reasoned. Of course, Grandpa's gun only shot little candies into the mouth; after all, it was the little toy gun he had given to his grandson, which he was borrowing for the occasion, but it certainly looked real enough.

He secured a hat and a pair of sunglasses.

With his trusty overcoat and wearing his podiatrist's specially-prescribed "support" sneakers, he walked into the noontime clamor of the local bank.

He handed the teller a note demanding money and then pushed aside his overcoat, ever so slightly, to reveal the gun. He had not loaded it with any candy this day.

The teller, naturally terrified, had done as she was told. She grabbed a fist full of hundred dollar bills and held them up.

"Give me the bag," she said.

"What?" asked grandpa.

"The bag for the money," repeated the teller.

"I don't have one," said Grandpa. Then, being a quick thinker, he said, "Get a bag for me." He indicated the gun. "And hurry."

The teller bent down and grabbed a small bag. As she did so, she slipped in a loaded pack of hundred dollar bills—called a "security pack." This pack, once activated, would explode in a continuous cloud of red smoke. She activated it as she put it in the pack.

"Now, don't move and don't make a sound," said Grandpa as he headed for the door.

Outside, his truck was waiting. He had parked it right in front of the bank. As he opened the door to his truck, the "security pack" in the bag exploded. Billowy clouds of red smoke poured out of the bag, covering Grandpa, painting him red. Grandpa started the truck and so he was not aware of the crowd of onlookers—some of whom were smart enough to jot down his license-plate number.

His truck careened down the street, red smoke billowing out the windows. Grandpa knew he was in trouble when he saw the police cars in hot pursuit. But, he kept going. After all, he was slipping and sliding down the mountain, but he still needed that custard pie in the face.

He got it soon enough.

Pulling into the parking lot of the local high school, red smoke pouring out of his truck, high school students craning their necks out of the windows to see what was going on, Grandpa decided to elude the police on foot. He abandoned his smoking vehicle and ran.

Well, "ran" isn't exactly the right word. Perhaps lumbered is a better one. After all, Grandpa was 5'6" tall and weighed 280 pounds.

So lumbering through the parking lot, to the hoots and hollers of America's teenage scholars, was this 280-pound RED person. He left red tracks on the pavement as he ran. Now up the hill he went, the cops on foot also.

At the top of the hill Grandpa clutched his chest and fell to the earth. The cops surrounded him.

"Pills," he croaked. "Get my pills." He indicated his pocket. Waves of laughter were coming from the high school, since this tableau was being played out within sight and earshot of the next generation. This was better than MTV. Nothing can get a chuckle out of a teenager like an adult making an ass of himself.

One cop reached into Grandpa's pocket, wiping his hand of the red stuff, before opening the pill box.

Grandpa took his pill. And the cops cuffed him and arrested him.

They arraigned him in the hospital in a wheelchair. Grandpa looked very old and tired and confused. They had bathed him in the hospital and he was no longer red, unless you count the scarlet blush of mortification that stained his soul.

Outside the hospital his wife and three grown children and his myriad grandchildren were trying to explain it all. Everyone was crying. Grownups, kids, even some spectators— the tears were flowing for the cameras.

"He's a good man," said his wife, "he was just stupid."

"Daddy was a good man, just stupid," said one of the grown children.

"Grandpa is just stupid," said one of the grandchildren.

"Stupid, stupid, stupid," the family chorused and cried for the cameras.

Grandpa, the patriarch of the clan, the master of all he surveyed, the dispenser of gifts, the man of luck, the man of respect, was now just a stupid, stupid, stupid old man. He pratfell his way down the mountain to the jeers of the young, but the inevitable custard pie had been lobbed into his face by his own family.

"Poor Grandpa," said his little grandson, shooting a candy into his mouth from the candy gun, "poor Grandpa, he was just stupid."

12

Oh, That Lucky Lorraine!

Lorraine DeBiteto was lucky, lucky, lucky. Three years ago, she won $40,000 at Tropworld in Atlantic City.

"I had invested a grand total of $50 of the $100 I had with me in the machine that day when Lady Luck smiled at me," she said. "I was in shock."

Then, a month later on her very next visit to the popular seaside resort, Lorraine hit for $12,000 at Bally's, Atlantic City.

"I had won $52,000 on the slots in two days. That's more than I make in a year at my job as a receptionist in the World Trade Center in Manhattan," said the 57-year-old widow and grandmother of two.

After taxes, Lorraine was left with approximately $35,000. She had to decide what to do with the money.

"My very first thought was to go out and buy stuff for everybody, my three daughters, my two grandchildren, myself. I actually made a list of everybody I was going to buy things for—expensive things, too. I really was . . . until. . . ."

. . . Until Lorraine's picture (her and a smiling casino executive both holding a giant check for $40,000) appeared in the local paper under the headline: "Oh, That Lucky Lorraine!"

The article that accompanied the picture recounted her double dose of luck in Atlantic City.

That's when the calls started coming in.

Ostensibly these were good luck calls from acquaintances and friends and local organizations and non-profit groups and various churches and individuals who had read about Lorraine's good fortune.

"All these calls had one thing in common. After wishing me the best, they asked for a donation. One person called, I had never met him before, and he wanted a handout. I told him to get a job. Other people wanted me to invest in various businesses. Some of the ministers who called told me that I had a God-given responsibility to support the church, their church. I told these people that I was Catholic and that I gave plenty to my own church. The calls actually lasted for a few weeks. Since then I've changed my number to an unlisted number. I'm just glad no one got my address."

Now Lorraine had been going to Atlantic City once a month for the past five years—before her incredible streak of luck hit. She estimated that she was down between four and six thousand dollars in that time. "I wasn't particularly lucky up until then. In fact, I would say that I was downright unlucky until then."

Lorraine hadn't bought any gifts when the calls started coming in and she was in too great a "state of shock" to go out and splurge during the telephone solicitation deluge. But it gave Lorraine time to think, time to assess her priorities. She realized that she was a generous woman and that her daughters and grandchildren had had gifts aplenty from her. It was time to think of herself.

"You know what I did?" she said. "I decided that what I really wanted to do with that money was play the slot machines, maybe even go to Atlantic City once a week instead of once a month. That's the most fun I have. I love a day trip to the casino, playing, having lunch, taking a stroll on the boardwalk. A weekly or twice-monthly trip would be wonderful. But I also didn't want to just give the money I had won all back—which is what I would do if I just played and played and played."

So Lorraine hit upon a plan.

She took $5,000 and put it in her regular bank account. "That was payback for my previous losses." Then, she divided her remaining $30,000.

"I decided that I wanted to be able to play for a very long, long time on that $30,000." In fact, Lorraine wanted it to last a gambling lifetime.

"I took $10,000 and put it into a 10-year CD. Then, I took another $10,000 and put that into a five-year CD. I then divided the final $10,000 into $2,000 increments and bought CD's for one, two, three and four years. That left me with $2,000 to play the first year with. I broke that up into $100 increments. Now, that's what I bring for my weekly trips—one hundred dollars. I have my yearly $2,000 divided into 20 individual stakes of $100. I play quarter machines that take two or three coins so my $100 lasts me. I limit my play to three hours or until I lose that $100. I play slowly. I play an hour, take a walk; play another hour, go have lunch; then another walk; then play a final hour. I pull the lever maybe three times a minute. Only once in the past two years have I actually lost the entire $100."

At the end of the first year, Lorraine had lost $1,200 of her $2,000 stake. She took the $800 and put it into a CD. Then she commenced play with the $2,000 that had matured on her one year CD. "I only used the $2,000 and I banked the interest," she said proudly. In subsequent years she plans to do the exact same thing.

So that's Lorraine's plan. She will play with a designated amount from that $30,000 that has been earmarked solely for gambling. And remember that that $30,000 represents a profit. By dividing it up and putting the bulk of it into CD's, Lorraine is actually making money on her win. She gets the benefits both of being frugal and of enjoying the gambling lifestyle. Playing this way, Lorraine could conceivably play a lifetime and never be a loser at the slots! How unlike poor Grandpa of the last chapter.

"If I were to ever hit another big jackpot, I would just increase my stake, as well as increase what I'm putting into the CD's. I might move up to dollar machines, if I had maybe $100,000 in winnings. Then I might even splurge and buy some gifts for the family," she laughed. "But this time I wouldn't be so anxious to have my picture taken."

Lorraine may never have another big win. Her mad tango with Lady Luck may be over. But her money-management scheme is sensible. She realizes that she loves playing the slots but she also doesn't want to lose what she's already won. By parceling out her playing money and getting interest on the rest, she is keeping that casino edge at bay. Yes, a hundred dollars is not a great session stake for many players and Lorraine's three hour-long playing sessions might not give everyone the level of action he or she requires. Still, Lorraine is a lucky woman, not because she hit it big twice, but because her common sense and self-discipline puts her in a rare category—someone who has not allowed the casinos to beat her. She may not have broken the one-armed bandits but she certainly has caused them severe sprains!

Unlike Grandpa of the previous chapter, Lorraine De-Biteto will not attempt to reach the gambling summit in one big climb. Slow and steady will be her pace . . . but then again, she'll never have to worry about that custard pie in the face!

13

Protect Yourself at All Times

Ripoffs, Scams and Slot Come-ons

You know everything there is to know about breaking the one-armed bandits. You know how the casinos think in placing their machines, you have a firm grasp of where the loose machines are most likely to be found in a casino, and you have sensible playing strategies for playing these machines. You know what areas of the country give you the best percentages and what denomination machines give you the best shot at coming home a winner.

Still, it's tough to win—even with all the information you have. The contest between you and the casino (and between you and yourself) is a rugged one, and often when Lady Luck smiles upon you, her twin sister, Dame Fortune, will suddenly become fickle and throw some chicanery your way.

There are two ways to lose your money in a casino. You can lose it at the machines because you've lost—or you can lose it at the machines because you've won and someone steals your winnings!

Generally, gambling writers are loaded with good advice about how to protect your money from the ravages of the hated and horrible HOUSE EDGE. We are always looking to protect as much of your precious bankroll from the casinos as we can. That's why we develop and/or look for the best strategies possible.

And that's a good thing.

But sometimes in our desire to protect you against the casinos we naively forget to warn you against an equally dangerous but even more insidious enemy—your fellow players. Or, rather, those casino predators who are dressed in player's clothing. These predators who are looking to make *your* money *their* score!

And these predators are legion. And you are their prey.

In almost every major casino, be it in Atlantic City or Las Vegas, Reno or Lake Tahoe, on an Indian reservation or a riverboat, there are crossroaders (a casino term that means THIEVES) who are looking to rip off, not just the casinos, but Y-O-U. They do so in many sundry and ingenious ways.

Yet, we rarely see methods for protecting ourselves against these nefarious denizens of America's pleasure domes. In fact, most of us are totally unaware of the presence of casino predators in our casino visits, unless we are unfortunate enough to discover that they have robbed us of our hard-earned bounty or even harder-earned wins.

Ever thought you won more than it turned out you had? "Gee, Sally, I could have sworn I won $500 and not $400." Ever see someone searching the floor for a supposedly lost chip? "I know I had four black chips. I must have dropped one."

The casinos are all too happy to keep us ignorant of the activities of these casino thieves because—well, how would the next commercial for the casino of your choice sound if the tag line was: "And we protect our patrons against cunning thieves, too!" You just might have second thoughts about going to a place that advertises it has thieves stalking the premises.

But where there is money, there is crime. It is a law of nature every bit as explosive as $E=MC^2$. So why would any intelligent human being think that casinos, places where millions of dollars change hands every day, would be immune from criminals and their works? In addition, so many glittering new casino venues have been plunked down in otherwise rundown and seedy neighborhoods to rehabilitate the area

without nary a thought to rehabilitating or, better yet, elimi-
nating the criminal element of the area in question. So crime
and criminals often thrive in the casino environment because
unwary and innocent casino patrons expose themselves to the
criminal's depredations, albeit unknowingly. Don't you be
one of the victims—it's difficult enough to walk away from a
casino with money in your pocket as it is.

Some of the crime around the casino is your garden
variety of street-type crime. Billy Ray has a good day at the
slots, and as he heads for his car, he's mugged and robbed by
several steely-eyed denizens of the underbelly of humanity
who had watched him cash in his load of coin at the cage.
Martha has her pocketbook lifted by a swift-footed nasty boy
in Nikes. James and Harriet's room was riffled while they
were taking a bath—at the machines.

Now, most of us know what steps have to be taken against
straight crime and street crime. Never leave money in your
room; put it in a safe deposit box. Don't leave the casino *alone*
with a *big win*. Leave the money with a friend, or at the cage,
and get your car and drive it to the front entrance and have a
security guard escort you into the car! Better yet, always use
valet parking where someone has to bring your car to you.
And keep your purse close to your heart, ladies, at all times.

But, what about *in* the casinos? What steps should you
take to protect yourself against coin scoopers, jackpot jumpers
and wallet lifters?

For you men, never keep your wallets in your pants'
pockets—especially your back pockets. Keep your wallets in
your shirts—in a *buttoned* pocket. If thieves want that wallet,
they are going to have to face you and rip it right out of your
shirt. Very few casino thieves are so daring. After all, a casino
is not a darkened alleyway, a deserted street or a dimly-lit
parking lot. And there is security, even though it's sometimes
just a tired old semi-retired guy with arthritis.

Always play the number of machines that you can watch
safely and easily because there are *scoopers* waiting to take
your quarters or dollar coins. These creeps will just walk by
you, pretending to be looking for an ash tray or a coin bucket
and when you're not looking (or even when you are), they
reach with one hand for the ashtray or coin bucket between

the machines you are playing and with the other hand they reach into your tray to scoop up as much coin as they can without drawing any attention to themselves. Most of the time, the slot player doesn't even know he's been ripped off.

Another type of scooper works with a partner. The partner distracts you—maybe he or she drops a whole bucket of coins on the floor right next to you. Being honest, you help this poor guy or gal pick up his or her loot, while the accomplice loots your tray or walks off with your fully-loaded bucket. You can find scoopers in almost every casino at almost any time of the day or night. Of course, like all criminals, they prefer to operate during the peak times, when the casinos are crowded and the players are cramped. Then they just reach in and take some coins as they casually walk by. You'd be surprised how many scoopers just walk and scoop, walk and scoop, through a casino and then they're out the door heading for their next targeted territory.

However, by far the worst kind of slot scoundrels are those individuals who try to rip off your jackpots. They have become quite subtle in this art. Rarely do they pretend that they won, disputing your claim to the jackpot, as was typical before the invention of video and the installation of cameras throughout the casino. Then, it was not unusual for a "claim jumper" to challenge your right to your jackpot. It would go something like this:

"I'm sorry, but this here lady is lying," states the claim jumper. "I put the coins in the machine, not her. She let me play because she was going to the bathroom. Now, because I won, she wants my jackpot! Hey, Frank! Hey, Frank! Didn't this here lady tell me that I could play this here machine until she got back from the bathroom?"

"Yup," says Frank, the accomplice. "She sure did, Jesse."

And suddenly you either lost your jackpot or had to share it with two thieves.

No, those days are blissfully over. The jackpot jumpers are much more devious now. Instead of disputing or challenging you, they befriend you.

Here's an awful but true story. Happened to an acquaintance of mine.

Josephine B. of Staten Island won a $1,200 jackpot at a slot machine. The coins poured out but most of the jackpot was to be paid by an attendant after Josephine gave him her name, address and other vital information. All during this, two very pleasant young ladies were congratulating Josephine on her good fortune. They even counseled her not to leave the machine until everything was paid to her and her win was in her purse. There were too many ripoff artists working the casinos, they cautioned her, so be wary.

Josephine was. She took her win and put it in her purse, just as her new "friends" had told her to.

Then one of the "friends" suggested she keep playing the machine because "this is your lucky day," and Josephine sat down to do so. With a "friend" on either side of her, Josephine began playing again. A few minutes later, the "friend" on Josephine's right got up to go to the bathroom. A few seconds later, so did the "friend" on the left.

Unfortunately, Josephine was not having a good time of it on this round of play and decided to reach for her purse to get some more money for the change girl. Her purse was gone. So were her new "friends" who had warned her about ripoff artists. Hmmm, where were those "friends" now?

It took Josephine several minutes to realize what had happened. Her two "friends" had done what friends do— shared in her good fortune. In fact, they totally *took* her good fortune!

The casinos are wonderful places to be, no doubt about it. But in today's world a new dictum joins the old "Let the buyer beware!" and that is "Let the player be wary!"

Learn from Lorraine

You should also learn a lesson from Lucky Lorraine of the previous chapter. If you hit a particularly big jackpot, one the smiling casino executives wish to photograph you for, perhaps you should consider passing up your five minutes of fame and just quietly pocket your winnings. I've spoken to a slew of big winners for this book and many of them regretted letting the casinos use their names and pictures in publicity brochures and press releases. Many were hounded by "well-wishers" trying to cash in on their luck. And the bigger the win, the better the chance that the winner will be inundated with requests to give it away! So pass up the publicity and pocket the profits!

Mail Order Schemes and Scams

As a slot player, you will often find yourself intrigued by advertising come-ons in both the regular and the gambling press.

You Can't Lose! Guaranteed Slot System!

You Too Can Make a Million Dollars Playing the Slots!

Slot Machine Secrets Revealed!

Incredible Breakthrough in Slots!

Slot Mechanic Reveals Little-Known Secret to Winning a Million!

Or you will receive brochures sent to your home stating that you are only one of 1,000 (or 2,000 or 5,000) people being given the opportunity to purchase "the key to opening the slot machine treasure." A good rule of thumb is this: If a promotion sounds too good to be true—it probably is!

No reputable gambling authority can *guarantee* you a win on any given night or even any given stretch of nights. Despite a clear mathematical advantage over the casino, a card-counter in blackjack isn't *guaranteed* a win; the Captain of craps himself can't guarantee that you'll definitely win your next session with his *Supersystem,* the most devastating way ever discovered to play the game of craps (see my book *Beat the Craps out of the Casinos: How to Play Craps and Win!)*—so how can anyone *guarantee* you a win at *slots?*

There are no foolproof systems either—because it is in the nature of a fool to screw up and misplay even the good systems of play that are available to him or her! Nothing made, invented or thought up by man can be *proofed* against a *fool.*

That's not to say that I don't think there are winning strategies available in many games—after all, I personally know many long-term winners, the Captain included. But this is just to say that no one can guarantee you a win on any particular occasion—unless that person is lying or trying to separate you from your hard-earned money by selling you some "secret" *guaranteed* to win you thousands.

Many of these come-ons are out-and-out scams—and expensive ones at that. Some of these come-ons simply offer—at an outrageous price—the traditional advice that can be found in outdated slot books about where to locate loose machines or how to manage your money when playing. These are often nothing more than cheap booklets or stapled photocopies, poorly written and edited, but expensively and extensively advertised and dearly bought by win-hungry and enthusiastic slot players. Some of these sell for as little as $30 while others go for as high as $1,000!

Some other come-ons are "get-rich-quick" schemes—for the sellers, that is! These are written with a sense of urgency. If you don't get in on the "secret" now—next week will be too late! The seller is withdrawing the offer at that time or after a certain number of people buy the "secret." So hurry, hurry, hurry!

One such mailing asks for a "down payment" of $25 against your first win—which is "guaranteed" the very first time you use the "secret" this authority sells. Then you send him $250 and keep all the millions you'll win for yourself! Wow! Of course, the authority isn't going to sell this secret to just anyone. He's looking for people who aren't rich. "I'm not interested in making the rich richer," he states. No, I think he's interested in making the poor soul who buys his secret $25 poorer! But what about that $250 you're supposed to send him when you win? Well, if this seller sells a few thousand "secrets," some of these suckers are bound to win on their very first outing—so, assuming these people are honest, they'll send along that $250. Our seller is banking on the fact that he'll get $25 from thousands of people and $250 from hundreds of people. Pretty ingenious, no?

All such promotions have one thing in common, however: The advertisements and mailings promise slot players the sun, the moon, the stars and a *guaranteed* win, while the actual "secret," when once revealed, delivers substantially less. In fact, the "secret" delivers essentially what is left over after food passes through a bull's digestive system. Here's an example of one such "secret" sold for an outrageous $300. The author of this "secret" tells you to look for mechanical slots and play them! Well, first, you will be hard-pressed to find any mechanical slots in a casino today. And, two, even if you did find some mechanical slots, that wouldn't guarantee you a win. After all, if these machines were defective, the casinos would have removed them long ago.

Some of these scams claim you can get your money back if you aren't "totally delighted" with the results. Of course, some of these scammers never even bother sending you anything at all—that's right, many of these "secret sellers" have a giant SECRET—they aren't selling ANYTHING but promises and hot air! Once they get a return on their advertisements, they just take your money and run. By the time you launch a complaint, the culprit has made off with your funds and the funds of all the other gullible slot players, leaving no forwarding address. However, more often than not, you will receive something from the "secret sellers," something that you may or may not decide to return. Interestingly enough, here's a BIG secret about the mail order business—very few people return what they purchase from system or secret sellers. Whether the buyers are embarrassed, lazy or stupid, the fact remains that the mail order return rate on gambling systems is quite low. That's just the way it is. So the seller can be fairly confident that he'll not be asked to make good on his money-back guarantee too many times.

The book you are reading right now contains the greatest secrets ever revealed about the slot machines and, therefore, you don't have to go hunting for the "holy grail of slot secrets" because you have already purchased it. So before you send away your hard-earned $300 to some scammer, reconsider: If you have a burning desire to mail that money to someone, why not mail it to me! And here is my guarantee—I will take every penny and use it in a casino!

Seriously, forget trying to purchase a secret that will make you a millionaire. I'll repeat—if it sounds too good to be true, it probably is!

Slot-Scamming the Casinos

Casinos also have to worry about con artists and cross-roaders ripping them off. In the bad old days of the mechanical and the electromechanical one-armed bandits, there were over 250 ways of cheating and beating the machines! Here's a list of the main categories of slot cheating in the past:

1. You could slam the handle.

2. You could walk the handle.

3. You could freeze the reels.

4. You could open the machine and set the reels.

5. You could put a spoon in the coin recepter.

6. You could jimmy the coin dispenser.

7. You could use slugs in the machine.

8. You could string the machine by putting a coin at the end of a string that could be used over and over.

9. You could ratchet the machine.

10. You could physically steal the machine from the casino.

11. You could tilt the machine.

12. You could pry open the coin box.

The most elaborate, and easy thing, was to drill a small hole in the machine and set the reels however you liked them! Whole slot aisles could be drilled by a professional team of crossroaders and before the casino knew what hit it, they'd be taking wheelbarrows of coins from the place.

But no more.

With the new computer-driven microprocessor machines, the old ways of cheating just don't cut it. As soon as a machine is tampered with—by drilling, spooning, slugging, etc.—an alarm is set off and simultaneously the machine shuts itself down. Thus, to cheat today's high-tech machines, you have to use high-tech cheating methods.

I have only heard of two high-tech assaults on the modern-day slot machine—both stories told me by third parties (although these particular parties have given me reliable information in the past) who got it from second parties who got it from the source. While both stories are sadly lacking any insider source I could talk to, I am sharing them with you for two reasons—they just might be true and they are definitely interesting (even if apocryphal).

One involved a group of airline employees who had supposedly figured out the sequencing codes and signals for many of the progressive jackpot prizes. According to my third-party source, these individuals have flown all over the world, winning jackpot after jackpot. "They never go for Megabucks or any of the jackpots that would draw big attention to them. And of course, the same individual doesn't win time and again. They spread the winning around so it looks like different people are winning all these jackpots. But all these different people belong to the same group."

The second story also involves a group—a group of surgeons. I guess with the high cost of malpractice these days, our surgeons were looking for something they could open up without fear of it suing them. Seems they used fiber optics to get inside the machines, just as they would use fiber optics to snake their way into an artery. Once inside the machine, they would find the payout "switch." However they did it, they were able to make the machine think that it hadn't paid out the last win. This win could be just a few coins, mind you, but the machine would keep spitting out those few coins until it emptied itself. Ingenious. According to my third-party source, the surgical team is still operating on their slot patients with deadly results.

I have to admit, I rather delight in stories such as the above. Tales of brilliant scams and colorful criminals always make for good reading. However, when I asked my sources within the slot manufacturing industry whether such scams were possible, they were skeptical. One executive stated: "The only way to [criminally] beat the slots is to affect the microprocessor chip and the only way to do that is at the source. You can open a machine and substitute a chip that changes the payout program. You might be able to do this inside a casino but it would be much easier to do it during the manufacturing process. So you would have to be an employee of the company. Then, you follow where the machine is sold and you send someone to play it the minute it's put on the floor. That would be about the only way to really sabotage the new slot machines."

Still, one executive left open the possibility that brilliant crossroaders might be able to "screw around with the machines without changing the chip or operating within the manufacturing process." He continued: "A chip can be electromagnetically made to malfunction. The problem would be to get it to malfunction in precisely the way you want it to. I think that's where a thief would have his problem. You could probably screw up the chip, but you would probably be unable to profit by it. Generally, with the programming we have, once a chip is tampered with or malfunctions on its own, for that matter, the whole shooting match shuts itself down."

Well, it's still fun to think about those airline people flying to glamorous places and winning jackpots wherever they go, or those brilliant surgeons painstakingly manipulating the latest in surgical techniques and equipment to get a slot machine to bleed to death. Perhaps the two groups should get together and call themselves *The Flying Slot Slicers.*

Anyway, whether the above stories are true or not, they offer a romantic conclusion to an otherwise serious and rather sad commentary on the state of honesty within the human gambling fraternity. May you beat the one-armed bandits but never have the misfortune of the human bandits beating you. Be wary. Be wise. And remember that as a player you must protect yourself at all times!

14

Superstitions, Stories and Statements

L et's have some fun.
From the interviews and slot surveys done for this book, my researchers and I stumbled upon some interesting ideas and superstitions and still more interesting slot-playing characters. Although our initial survey of 2,000 players yielded disappointing results (to say the least), still there were some golden nuggets of information, insights, and rather bizarre intuitions scattered throughout.

So meet some of the people and enjoy some of their ideas. Here they are in their own words. Some of these individuals were obviously talking with tongues firmly planted in cheeks, others weren't. Some had colorful nicknames for their gambling personas (generally given to them by themselves). I hope you enjoy them.

Leonora of Staten Island, New York: I walk around the casino at least three times before I decide on what machine to play. I always pick a machine that has the coin light on top of it flashing but no one is playing the machine. I think this signal is my lucky signal. When I sit down a change person is almost immediately available. I don't have to wait. That light is my signal to play.

Patricia of Nevada: I play the slots until I lose all my money. But I only bring $20. I would probably lose everything if I brought everything. My friend Vicki will play for 24 straight hours on the weekends. She'd rather play slots than have sex. Vicki's husband ran away with a dealer and she didn't even know it for a week. He left a note and she didn't find it for a week. Vicki is a slot maniac.

Bulletman of Inwood, New York: I have the secret of slot playing. This is the *Bulletman's Secret of Slot Playing.* I use this technique all the time and I've been very successful with it. You see, the reason people don't win at the slots is because they get headaches and it screws up their concentration so they don't know what the hell they're doing. These headaches are caused by the spinning reels—especially the bars. So when I put my quarters in—and I always play maximum coin—I put my head down and wait for the decision when the reels stop spinning. I've been able to increase my time at the slots this way and avoid headaches. I've saved quite a bit of money because I haven't had to buy painkillers when I go to the casino.

Raymon of Arizona: I am a teacher of music. I can tell you that all things contain a life force, although all life forces are not the same. The life force of a musical instrument is in harmony with man, while the life force of a gun or a car is not. The slot machine has a life force that can be harmful. It is seductive and destructive. I play because I am drawn to play. I believe that they are alive with their own kind of life. The slot machine has a vampire life force.

The Rancher of Dallas, Texas: Like is to like. You feel the machine and if it's hot, you can heat up your coins with a lighter or rub them with your hands to make them warm and put them in. But be careful when you use a lighter because those coins heat up fast and you can get severe burns. If the machine is cold, you put the coins in your ice water and cool them off and then put them in. Dry them first, however. When you go to a machine you have to touch it and get a feel for its condition. I put my cheek against it. You play like to like. This is a secret way of playing that I bought from someone. Oh, no, I haven't won any money, except once in a while—but what the heck.

Elizabeth of Garciasville, Texas: I start with $10 and if I win I keep playing with the coins that I've won. Of course, this is my first time in Las Vegas. I'm playing the slots because I don't know how to play the table games. I just won $200 so maybe I should quit forever and be a winner.

Tracie of Newark, New Jersey: I'm Tracie with an I-E and i.e., I haven't won a damn thing at these infernal machines! But I love playing them. Remember that's I-E.

Ann of Los Angeles, California: I don't play table games because after each play I like to count up my chips and know exactly what I have. But that slows down the games so the other players get hissy. At the slots, I take my time and add my money up whenever I want for as slow as I want. I just give myself a certain amount to play with and when it's done it's done . . . well, sometimes.

Joe of Pittsburgh, Pennsylvania: I only play dented machines. I've had my best luck on dented machines. I don't dent them myself but I figure if it's dented on the outside, it might be screwed up on the inside. I can't wait to find a dented Megabucks machine because then I'll be rich.

Michael of New Orleans, Louisiana: There's no way to beat the machines, none at all. You have to be a crazy man to play them. They are purposefully designed to take your money. You have to be out of your mind to play them. I go over to Biloxi every week and play them like crazy. So I guess I'm out of my mind. But it's fun.

Barry of Columbia, Maryland: I fall asleep at the slots. I sit, put a few coins in, and before you know it I'm asleep. My wife comes over and wakes me up. Once I fell asleep as the machine was spinning and I woke up with a tray full of coins. I didn't even know I won until I heard my wife scolding me that someone could have just robbed me of my jackpot and I wouldn't have known the difference.

Boots of Arkansas: Ah jus kick 'em once or twice jus' to let 'em know who's boss. 'Course, thay don' ever lissin.

Howard of Queens, New York: Don't even talk to me about the slots. I don't really want to talk about them because I have nothing interesting to say about them, really. Really, what can I say that hasn't been said before? I don't think you can beat them. I play because I like the idea of having a shot at some big money. It also passes the time. I'm retired, you know, owned a shoe business, then a dress shop, but now. . . . You know, what is there to say, really? You go to Atlantic City and you play and then you come home and you're probably broke. But I only take a certain amount. I've got two friends and we go once a week. It's something to do. I really don't have anything to say because what is there to all of it? You put in coins and press the button. I play one coin at a time. I can play all day doing one coin at a time. One coin. One coin. One coin. I've lost three coins but my friends have lost a dozen or more. They lose so much the casino gives them lunch for two and so we have lunch for four but there's only three of us so I get a free lunch when I go and I don't really play for very much. We order enough for four and have the waitress wrap everything up. So when I go home I have dinner too. And I play only one coin. I like the winters better than the summers in Atlantic City. There's really not that much to say about the slots.

Marian of San Diego, California: Oh, I'm not a big player. I take $500 for the weekend and I play $50 at one casino, then $50 at another, then 50 at another. I like to walk from casino to casino on the Strip. I've actually lost weight walking up and down the Strip. Unfortunately, I've lost money too.

Kid Nostrils of Atlantic City, New Jersey: Man, I can smell when a machine is ready to hit the big one. I think the wiring gets hot because they'll be pumping a signal through the lines that says to the machine: "Get hot, buster." Well, I walk around sniffin' the air around a machine because I got the most sensitive nose there is. When I smell that certain machine-smell, I just start playing. When my nose is workin' right, I never lose. I'm only losing today because I got a cold.

John of Corona, California: The lady right next to me last night won a huge jackpot. A guy a few machines down did too. The last time I came someone hit for a progressive down the aisle from me. I seem to be surrounded by winners whenever I go. But I always lose. The best way to select a machine would be to find me and play a machine a few feet from me. You'd probably be guaranteed a win. People should actually pay me to come to a casino so they can sit near me and win a fortune. Maybe I should go into business. You think I could make some money that way?

Buddy of Brooklyn, New York: I once punched a machine. I punched it with all my strength and broke the middle knuckle of my right hand. That machine was so cold, so I punched it. After I got my hand fixed, I went back to that same machine and some woman was winning a fortune on it. I felt like punching her too.

David of Chicago, Illinois: I know everyone says that the machines are random, but I don't believe it. I think there is a special switch or a signal that a casino boss can press or send that tells a machine to start paying off. If they like you, they'll let you win. If they don't like you, they make you lose. I try to get real friendly with the casino personnel because I figure sooner or later one of them is going to like me and let me hit the big one. Of course, these casino people are so busy that I just don't get to talk to them much. They always seem to be rushing off whenever I really get into a good conversation with them.

Bunti of Malverne, New York: I once talked with an elderly lady and she told me why people play the slots when they're her age. She said she had the usual ups and downs of living. She raised her family and she and her husband both worked very hard. She first worked as a housewife but when her children were grown, she went to work in a bank. When the first televisions came out, they saved up and bought one. Same with the color televisions. Then, as their family grew, they bought a much larger refrigerator. Each year there was always something to save for or something to look forward to. She told me all she wanted now was a bigger bucket to put her wins in. Her husband had died several years ago. Her children live out of state. Her goal now was to start with a small bucket and move to a bigger one. That was her life now.

Sal of America: I'm an American through and through. I fought for my country in 'Nam and I'd fight again if they called me. Of course, I'm about a hundred pounds overweight and my blood pressure is through the roof and my eyes ain't worth crap, but I think of myself as a patriot. So America, that's where I'm at. So I'm just Sal from America. Call me that when you identify me. Sal from America or Sal, the American. Or Big Sal, the patriot. Because that's me. That's me. I sit here and look around this casino and you see all this money? Well, that's America. People work hard, make a good living, spend some money on fun. Eat and raise a family. That's what it's all about for me and every American. Everyone here is here to have a good time. What's so bad about that? Nothin'. We shouldn't feel guilty because we want to have a good time. When you're in the box and they're shovelin' dirt on you, what are you gonna say: "Hey, I didn't spend my money on fun. I lived miserably and now I'm worm meat?" So, you gotta have fun, that's what I'm saying. Me? I *never* play the slots. I don't gam-

SUPERSTITIONS, STORIES, AND STATEMENTS

ble. I'm just mindin' this one for my wife. She's a nut when it comes to the slots. This machine here she figures is *her* machine. She won't let no one touch it. She would kill me if she thought I'd let anyone play it. She's got her mother's temper. You know that case where the wife cut off her husband's you-know-what? Well, that's what my wife would do to me if I let anyone play her machine. She's been losin' all day on this one but she figures it's gonna hit soon. I hope so because we're losin' a bundle!

Speedy of Boston, Massachusetts: I put the coins in really slow. One. Two. Three. Then I pull down the handle really slow. I think if you pull the handle fast, the machine misses a beat and you might skip over the winning sequence. So I pull real slow. Now, I have a friend that insists it's the other way around. That you have to pull the handle with lightning speed because as the coins register the machine automatically goes through the winning sequences first so that the faster you pull the handle the better your chances for winning. I think he's wrong. The winning sequences are at the end so you pull the handle real slow and you have a much better chance of winning. Actually, we've both lost about the same amount on the machines so who knows what's the right way to play them?

Tess of Brooklyn, New York: Do you think it's blasphemous that I go to church every morning on a day when I go to the casino? I pray to God to give me a big win. I know some religions frown on gambling but I just love to go to Atlantic City and Connecticut to play. You see these? That's St. Jude, the patron saint of lost causes, and the other is the Sacred Heart. I put them both in the tray to give me luck. One on each side. I have a rosary and scapula in my purse. So far I've been pretty lucky, at least compared to some of my friends.

William of Las Vegas, Nevada: I don't like people. Really. I never married. I work a night job where I almost never see a human being. I don't play table games because I can't stand the people at the table games. To me the casino is the safest place in the world. I sit at a machine and play a few days a week. It's fun. No hassles. Actually I consider the casino to be my home away from home. No, I'm never lonely.

Diamond Dallas of Dallas, Texas: I made all my money in oil—corn oil! I own a grocery store outside Dallas, actually. I come to Mississippi now a lot. I like it better than Las Vegas—it's a little cheaper for me and my wife to get there and back. I have figured a way to tell if I'm going to win on a riverboat. I check out the hull of the boat. If it's sitting low in the water then I figure there's a ton of coin in the machines and they're ready to explode—either that or the ship will sink!

15

Oh Yes, It's the IRS!

Gambling is fun and winning is even more fun. And when you win big, it's the greatest fun of all. But just as you are celebrating your big win and people are slapping you on the back and you're dreaming of how you're going to spend all that money you just won, a casino employee will give you the bad news.

"Sir (or Madam), you'll have to fill out some forms for the IRS and I'll need to see some identification and your social security number."

Oh yes, whenever you win in a casino, you suddenly discover that you have some partners. In table games, the partner is always the casino itself, since the casino keeps a percentage of all wins in the form of the vig or vigorish. In slots, if you win $1,200 or more, the government becomes your partner and you are expected to pay taxes on the money that you've won.

You will be given a W-2G form—"Statement from Certain Gambling Winnings." Copy A will be sent by the casino to the Internal Revenue Service and Copy B will be given to you to file with your yearly income tax. Rarely does the IRS withhold any tax money at the time of your winning. However, come tax time you will be expected to include your slot winnings as a part of this year's earned income and pay your taxes on them as if they had been income.

However, there is a slight ray of sunshine in this rather bleak party-pooping, because the IRS allows you to deduct this year's losses from this year's winnings but *only up to the amount lost* and only if you itemize your deductions. You may have been losing for the past five years, losing bundles and bundles of money, but if you should be ahead this particular year in which you won a big jackpot, the IRS has no provision to carry over the losses of previous years to offset this year's win. So one great win, even in a lifetime of horrendous losing, is suddenly diminished because the government wants a piece of the action. The chances of this particular injustice being changed are remote, since no member of Congress seems overly interested in championing the rights of gamblers to a fair shake.

There are, however, ways to assure yourself the best of a bleak situation should you be lucky enough to have a winning year but unlucky enough to have the IRS in on the party. Since you can deduct the losses you sustained in the year of your great win, you have to keep accurate records of your playing. Sad but true, the bureaucracy reaches even into your gambling life, because you should be able to prove all the occasions that you went to a casino, how many hours you played, how much you won or lost. You should keep your hotel or motel receipts, your airline or bus receipts, your credit card receipts, your markers, and perhaps even a diary that outlines your daily activities while in the casino. These will be acceptable proofs for most IRS agents in the event you have to defend your losses against a big win.

Thankfully, here the casino, which acts as an unwilling agent of the IRS in reporting your winnings, can act as your agent as well. If you belong to a slot club, the casino has a detailed account of your slot play in their casino. Whenever you have a year with an IRS-alerting big win, you should request that the casinos you patronize verify your total play for the IRS. They can do this simply by providing a computer-generated spread sheet of your play. Or they can do this by filling out a "Statement of Loss" form. Of course, you have to take the good with the bad and it is possible that if you're having a winning year all around, you'll be paying even more in taxes once the casino verifies your action. But that's the chance you have to take.

So death and taxes are still the two things you can't escape. Even though you might be fortunate enough to break the one-armed bandits, you might find yourself faced with the dismal prospect of protecting yourself against some two-armed types trying to horn in on your score. Isn't that always the way of things?

16

A Final Word

Slot playing is here to stay. I have no doubt about that. And why not? It's obvious that people enjoy "those infernal machines" and like the challenge of trying to break the one-armed bandits.

If playing the slots gives you pleasure and the price of that pleasure isn't too steep (as it was with poor grandpa), then why shouldn't you enjoy yourself? Why shouldn't you eagerly anticipate your next outing to the casino of your choice? Why shouldn't you pull that handle and press that button, if pulling and pressing are your pleasures?

If you're reading this book, I think you are probably the type of person who is in control of yourself. By the way, I don't think people who read gaming books are the type of people who tend to go on tilt ("going on tilt" means losing control) in the casinos or the type who are compulsive gamblers. Compulsive types are too busy fueling and stoking the fires of their compulsions to reflect on what they're doing. After all, reading a book takes time and effort—the time and effort a compulsive type doesn't want to waste on anything save his or her compulsion. Reading about gaming for many people is almost as much fun as actually doing it—at least I find it so.

For more and more people, gaming has become the hobby of choice: It's exciting and offers a change of pace from the humdrum workaday world that most of us live in. After all, casinos are certainly exciting and glamorous places, for the most part. As gaming becomes ever more popular with the general public and as that public becomes ever more learned and astute, casinos will be forced (I hope) to give better games and better paybacks on already existing games such as the slot machines. Of course, you might be able to rush this day along by patronizing only those casinos that give you the best deal. If you are an Atlantic City player, for example, go to the casinos whose statistics give you the best game at the denomination you've chosen to play. The other casinos will wise up as they see their competitor locking up that denomination's market. Then they'll offer better games, we hope.

Without question, the most fun of all is winning. Just because your chosen game is the one-armed bandit doesn't mean that you must resign yourself to losing time and time again when you go to a casino. It may very well be that in the long run you will suffer the fate of most gamblers—and lose. But you can approach that fate in either one of two ways: resignedly or . . . KICKING AND SCREAMING!

I prefer that you go kicking and screaming!

So, slot players, you should play to win! Get all the comps you can get. Look for loose machines. Play the best playing strategies. Follow the advice of the Hildebrands and the Captains and the Julians and of that Lucky Lorraine as I've set it down in this and other books. Learn from Mr. Handle, too, because he has shown you how the casinos think.

In point of fact, I don't think any wise player is *fated* to lose—even if your game is slots. We now know that with a 99-percent machine and a one-percent-of-total-play comping philosophy, it is theoretically possible to break even at the slots—the rub is to locate those 99 percenters. Perhaps that could be extended to the 98-percent machines as well. In Las Vegas, you could certainly realistically entertain the hope of breaking even in the long run on such machines—as long as you average your comps in with your slot play. Then, with a little luck—maybe a nice lifetime supply of jackpots (such as Lorraine's)—and you can have your cake and eat it too. Or, rather, have your slots and beat 'em too!

The slot player does live on hope, certainly, it's his staple diet. It's what energizes him. But there's realistic hope and unrealistic hope. Figuring you're going to win Megabucks because "someone will win it and it might as well be me" is unrealistic hope. Yes, some ONE PERSON will win that jackpot you're looking at. However, some MILLIONS OF PEOPLE will lose pursuing that same jackpot—and they'll lose a lot and that's why that particular jackpot is so BIG. So it's an unrealistic hope that you'll be the one out of the millions of players who'll win. Don't get suckered in. If you must play a progressive, then make it an in-house progressive. But, better still, avoid the progressives and go for the best machines as defined in this book.

Be realistic. If you want to play the slot machines for a long time, you can't allow yourself to get clobbered every time you go to a casino. That's certainly no one's definition of fun. So look for the loose machines as outlined by Mr. Handle and play the best strategies as outlined in various sections of this book. If you do this, you have a realistic hope of winning. There are no guarantees that you can break the one-armed bandits, but there is realistic hope that you can do so. Remember this, too—that when Pandora opened the box and allowed all the evils of the world to cascade out, there was only one good thing that escaped with them—hope!

I think this book has given you a realistic hope of beating the slot machines. So, what are you waiting for? Go out and break those one-armed bandits!

And good luck!

Glossary

Ace Lock: Brand name for a high security lock found on many slot machines that uses a cylindrical key.

Action: The amount of money you wager over a given period of time. Used as a basis of judgment for comps.

Action Player: A player who bets big and for long periods of time. Sometimes used as a euphemism for stupid player.

Adjustable Jackpot: The money compartments of the machine can be adjusted to accommodate a greater or lesser number of coins.

Automatic Payout: Direct payment from the machine to the player without the need of a slot attendant's assistance.

Award Card: Same as *payout card, payment panel, reward card, reward panel.* The posted payouts for the various symbol combinations of a given machine.

Back Bonnet: Protective covering in the upper rear portion of a machine.

Back Lip: Protective plate that covers the coin entry area.

Bad Rack: Casinoese for a player who doesn't pay his gambling debts.

Bank: The person who covers the bet in a game. In most casino gambling, the bank is the casino itself. Also, a row of slot machines.

Bankroll: The total amount of money a gambler sets aside to gamble with.

Bar: The banning of an individual from playing in a casino. Used against cheats and expert players alike. Also, one of the symbols on a slot reel.

Big Bertha: Those giant slot machines placed at entrances and exits to lure the unwary gambler. Not one of the better machines to play.

Big Player: At slots, a player who plays for a sufficient amount of time at a relatively high-denomination machine.

Both-Way Payout: The paying symbol combinations can be read from left to right or from right to left.

Bust Out Joint: A casino that cheats the players.

Buy Bet: To buy the point numbers four and 10 by paying a five percent commission.

Bug: Sometimes euphemistically called an "odds adjuster." A mechanical contrivance that can be placed on a mechanical slot machine to prevent a given symbol from appearing.

Buy-A-Pay Machines: A machine where multiple coins must be played in order to "buy" a higher and more varied-symbol return.

Cage: The cashiers' area of a casino where chips are exchanged for cash.

Cancel Button: The button in video poker that allows a player to cancel the previous choice(s) made.

Carousel: The name for an area containing a group of slot machines, usually of the same type, serviced by an individual cashier. Sometimes in a circular arrangement.

Cash Box: The removable container that accumulates coins.

Cash Out Button: The button on a machine that allows you to receive the coins that a machine has credited you with.

Casino Advantage: The edge, usually shown as a percentage, that the house has over the player.

Casino Host: The person responsible for seeing that high rollers are treated with the dignity and graciousness their wallets merit.

Casino Manager: The person responsible for seeing that the games of a given casino are handled properly.

Change Person: Individual who changes currency for coin in the slot areas.

Chasing Losses: Increasing your bets in order to recoup what you've lost. Not a good way to play.

Check: Also known as a *token*. The coin that is individually made for each casino that represents the dollar, five-dollar and higher denominations.

Choppy Game: A game where neither the house nor the player has been winning consistently. Opposite of a streak.

Cigarette Reel Strips: Reel strips with cigarette packs as stops. These were used as trade stimulators at the turn of the century.

Claw Machine: A novelty machine that allows a person to operate a mechanical claw in order to push or scoop coins.

Clocking: Keeping track of the results of a particular game.

Coin Return: A feature on slot machines that returns either bent coins, tokens from another casino, or slugs to the player.

Comps: The "freebies" that casinos give out for certain levels of betting.

Cradle: Sometimes referred to as the "sensing cradle." Where newly played coins come to rest for the purposes of "sensing." If coin is present and acceptable, play will proceed.

Credit Button: The button that allows the player to play winning credits and not coin.

Credit Line: The amount of credit a player is allowed by a given casino.

Credit Manager: The person in charge of determining casino credit for a player.

Criss-Cross: A machine that rewards play when the bars are on a diagonal or are showing on any other non-paying position.

Crossroader: A casino cheat.

Deal Button: In video poker, the button that is pushed to get the machine to "deal" the cards.

Denomination: A machine's classification based upon what type of coin is required to play it.

Desperado: A gambler who plays foolishly, usually chasing his losses.

Double Progressive Slots: Two different progressive slot jackpots on the same machines, each growing independently. Jackpots alternate based on pull of the handle or press of the button.

Double-Up Slot Machine: A two-coin multiplier that doubles the size of the payouts for the second coin. Will usually include a jackpot for the second coin played.

Double-Up System: This is also known as the Martingale family of wagers. Player attempts to get all his previous losses back by increasing (doubling) his previous bet.

Draw: In video poker, to receive new cards.

Draw Button: The button on a video-poker machine that allows a player to receive another card.

Drilling: A cheating method whereby the cheat drills a hole in the machine in order to manipulate or freeze the reels in a jackpot position.

Dummy Symbol: A slot machine symbol that is gaffed not to actually show on a payout line.

Dumping: A machine that is paying out much more than its programming dictates at a particular time. A machine that is losing money for the casino over a short period of time is said to be "dumping."

Electromechanical Slot Machine: A slot machine that utilizes both electrical and mechanical elements for its performance.

Edge: The advantage in a game.

Eighty-six: The same as barring someone from playing in the casino.

Escalator: A device that displays, usually for identification of slugs, the coins most recently put into the machine.

Even Up: A bet that has no mathematical edge for either side.

Even Money: A bet that pays off at one to one.

Eye in the Sky: The cameras, usually in bubbles, located throughout the casino that videotape the action.

Fair Game: A game where neither the house nor the player has an edge.

Five-Line Pay: A payout scheme which allows the player to win on up to three horizontal and two diagonal paylines per play by putting a coin in for each payline the player wishes to play.

Fluctuation in Probability: Numbers or sequences on a slot machine appearing out of proportion to their probability. A short sequence of repeating numbers. A mathematical term that means good or bad luck depending on whether the fluctuation is in your favor or not.

Free Play: To be able to play a slot machine without having to put in a coin.

Front Money: Money previously deposited with the cage and used by the player to draw markers against.

Fruit Machine: The slot machines that use fruit symbols.

Fun Book: Coupon book used by casinos to encourage play. Can be used to get an advantage at certain games if two players pool money and bet opposite sides. Also, it contains discounts for drinks, food, etc., or special payouts at the machines.

Future Pay Machines: A type of machine that holds back the payout until the next spin of the reels.

Gaffed: Any gaming device that has been rigged.

Gambling Stake: Amount of money reserved for gambling. Same as *bankroll.*

George: A good tipper.

Ghost: A stop on a slot machine reel that is blank.

Graveyard Shift: The 2 a.m. to 10 a.m. working shift in a casino.

Grifter: A scam artist.

Grind: Derogatory term for low roller. A small money player.

Grind Down: The casino winning all of a player's money due to the advantage it has on bets.

Grind Joint: A casino that caters to low rollers.

Grind System: Increasing one's bet by a unit after each win. Also, any system that attempts to win small amounts frequently against the casinos.

Guerrilla Gambling: The combination of smart play and hit-and-run tactics to beat the casinos at their own games.

High Roller: A player who plays for large stakes.

Hold: The actual amount that the casinos take from their games.

Hold Button: In video poker, the button that allows you to keep certain cards.

Hopper: Electronically powered payout system that counts out the coins to be paid accurately and fast. Some people also use the term hopper to refer to the tray that catches the coins.

Hot: A player who has been winning.

Hot and Cold System: A wager on the side that won previously. Another name for the streak method of betting.

Hot Machine: A machine that is paying off more than it's taking in.

House Edge: The mathematical edge that the casino has on a given bet.

House Odds: The payoff that reflects the casino's tax on your winning bet.

Hustler: A gambling cheat.

Irregularity: A departure from the standard procedures at a given game. A machine that is malfunctioning.

Jackpot: A grand payout, either on a machine or at a table game, with a low probability of occurrence.

Jackpot Jumpers: Name for thieves who attempt to steal your jackpot either by claiming it was theirs or by befriending you and making off with your money when you least suspect it.

Jackpot-Only Machines: A machine that has relatively large payouts with relatively infrequent occurrence. These machines usually contain many ghost sections.

Johnson Act: A federal law that forbids the shipment of gambling devices except to states that can operate them legally. Act took effect on January 3, 1951.

Junket: A trip arranged, organized and subsidized by a casino to bring gamblers to play at the games.

Junket Master: The person in charge of a junket.

Kibitzer: An individual who is not playing at a given game but is giving unwanted advice.

Liberty Bell: The original slot machine invented by Charles Fey.

Light-Up Slot Machines: First created by the Jennings Company. Machines that have electronically lit panels.

Lightning Slot Machines: Jackpot-only machines that pay out a lot of coin rapidly.

Long Run: The concept that a player could play so often that probability would tend to even out. That is, you would start to see the total appearance of numbers approximating what probability theory predicts. In slot machines, the long run would reflect the programming of the machine's probabilities and payouts. A long run player is a player who plays a lot!

Loose Machine: A slot machine or video poker machine that is paying off more than other machines of its type. A machine that is winning for a player.

Mark: An individual who has been or is going to be cheated. A sucker.

Megabucks: Giant inter-casino linked-progressive dollar slot machine that can pay a huge jackpot for three coins played.

Mechanical Machine: The oldest form of slot machine. Ran by gears, pulleys and levers. The handle was the direct cause of all that happened inside the machine.

Microprocessor Machines: The modern, computerized "smart" slots, where a microprocessor computer chip controls and simulates the play-action of a traditional slot machine.

Mills Machines: The first slot machines to use fruit symbols and to pay out a jackpot.

Money Management: The methods a player uses to conserve his bankroll from ruin.

Multiple-Coin Machines (Multipliers): Machines that require multiple coins to be played to win the best payouts.

Multiple-Pay Machines: Machines that pay out on more than one line depending on how many coins are played.

Nail: To catch someone cheating. "We nailed him."

Negative Progression: Any system of wagering where you increase bets after a loss.

Nevada Nickels: Giant, inter-casino linked progressive where the play of three nickels can lead to a giant jackpot win.

Nut: The total amount of money needed to run a casino or the total amount of money an individual needs to succeed at what he is doing.

Odds: The likelihood of a given event happening.

One-Armed Bandits: The term given to slot machines during a time when they were sold and distributed by less-than-reputable individuals.

On the Square: A game that is honest.

Parlay: To double one's bet after a win.

Payline: The line upon which a player is paid at slots. Generally corresponds to the number of coins played.

Payout Meter: A numerical counter with a visible display that keeps a running count of the coins played and paid out after each win.

Payout Percentage: The percentage of the money played that is returned to the player.

P.C.: The house edge expressed as a percentage.

Penny Ante: A game played for small stakes.

Playing Cycle: The sequence of events that occurs from the moment a player puts in the coins to the stopping of the reels and the paying of any monies won.

Power of the Pen (or Pencil): The ability of some casino executives to issue hotel comps to players.

Premium Players: A casino term meaning big bettors or players with big credit lines.

Producer: Casino term for a player who loses often and for large sums. This individual is a producer of profits for the casino.

Progressive Jackpots: The grand prize offered on certain kinds of slot and video poker machines that keeps growing as more and more money is played. Grows until it is hit by a player.

Push: Casinoese for tie.

Pushing the House or *Pushing the Casino:* The term coined by the Captain to describe a player in the act of getting a better game from a casino than advertised.

Quartermania: Giant inter-casino linked-progressive slot system that pays a huge jackpot for two quarters.

Quarter Player: Player whose play is exclusively on the 25-cent machines.

Random Number Generator: Sometimes referred to as RNG. The computer program that generates a series of random numbers. In the microprocessor machines, each sequence of random numbers will correspond to some predetermined sequence on the reels.

Rating: Evaluating a player's play for the purpose of comps.

Rating Card: The card used for rating a player. Most slot clubs will give you a card that can be placed in the machine so the casino can keep track of your play.

Reel: One of the loops inside a slot machine upon which the symbols are painted.

Reel Window: The glass display area that shows the reels.

Rhythm Play: Antiquated mechanical-slot-machine-playing method of rhythmically playing the machines by manipulating the handles to enhance one's ability to hit certain payouts.

RFB: Complimentary room, food and beverage.

Ruin or Element of Ruin: Losing your bankroll. The probability of losing every penny of your bankroll.

Rule Card: The card that shows the rules for a given game or for a tournament.

Rush: A quick winning streak.

Scam: Any scheme to defraud a casino or player. For slot players these scams usually involve guarantees that you can beat the machines if you use a "secret" method only known to the scammer.

Scared Money: Money a player can't afford to lose. Also known as *perspiration pennies.*

Session: A given period of play at a casino. Usually terminated at a predetermined time or at a certain level of wins or losses.

Shift Boss: The individual in charge of the casino during a given work shift.

Shill: An individual employed by the casino to play games that are being underplayed. It was not unusual in the past, when slot machines were not the game of preference for casino gamblers, that shills would sit at a machine and proclaim how much they had won on this bank of machines. This practice isn't necessary anymore.

Short Odds: Less than the true odds payoff of a bet.

Short Run: The limited amount of time during any given session when probability theory will seemingly be skewered by streaks or fluctuations.

Slot Arcade: A casino devoted exclusively to slot machines.

Slot Floor: Areas devoted to slot machines in a casino.

Slot Mix: Slot machines of different denominations and of different percentages in the slot area.

Slug: A piece of rounded metal inserted into a slot machine that mimics a coin. At one time slugging was a preferred way of illegally beating the machines. New machines can sense slugs and will shut down or reject the slug.

Spooning: Sticking a spoon into a slot machine to get it to pay off. Doesn't work any more with the new machines.

Steaming: A player who is visibly upset and is playing recklessly.

Stops: The various points where a slot reel might become stationary.

Straight Slots: Slots that have an unvarying payout. Non-progressive.

Stringing: A method of cheating whereby a coin or slug suspended on a string is introduced time and again into a machine in order to get free play.

The Strip: Las Vegas Boulevard. Three miles of casinos.

Swing Shift: The shift that runs from 6 p.m. to 2 a.m.

Tandem Slot Machines: A pair of slot machines coupled to the same handle. You have to place coin(s) in both machines before you can pull the handle.

Tapped Out: Having lost one's entire bankroll.

Ten-Stop Slot Machine: A slot machine with 10 stops for each of its reels.

Three-Line Payout: Depending on the number of coins inserted, payouts can be on one, two or three lines.

Tight Machine: A slot machine that is not paying back a good percentage. A machine at which a player is losing.

Tilting: Any physical manipulation of a machine during play in order to influence the outcome.

Toke: A tip to a casino employee.

Token: See *Check*.

Tom: Casinoese for a poor tipper.

Tough Out: The Captain's term for a skilled player who doesn't beat himself.

Trade Stimulator: Slot machines in stores that were there to increase sales of products.

Twenty-One Bell: The lining up of three sevens. It pays a jackpot.

Twenty-Stop Slot Machine: Each reel has twenty individual stops.

Two-For-One: A player gets two pulls of the handle for one coin.

Underground Joint: An illegal casino.

Vic: A sucker. Short for victim.

Video Slot Machine: The use of a video display to simulate the spinning of reels.

Vig or Vigorish: The casino tax on a bet. Also known as *juice.*

Virgin Principle: The superstition that a beginner will have luck. Also known as *beginner's luck.*

Wager: Another term for a bet.

Walking the Reels: An old method of cheating whereby a mechanical machine's handle could be used to manipulate reels into jackpot positions.

Wash: One bet cancels out another bet.

Wild Symbol: A symbol that can be substituted for any other symbol on a slot machine.

Index

Best Bets from Bonus Books

Beat the Craps out of the Casinos
How to play craps and win
Frank Scoblete
ISBN 0-929387-34-1
152 pages—paper—$9.95

Guerrilla Gambling
How to beat the casinos at their own games
Frank Scoblete
ISBN 1-56625-027-7
339 pages—paper—$12.95

Workouts and Maidens
Inside betting info for those who want to win at the track
Vincent Reo
ISBN 1-56625-000-5
180 pages—paper—$11.95

Finding HOT Horses
Pick horses that can win for you
Vincent Reo
ISBN 0-929387-96-1
135 pages—paper—$12.00

Overlay, Overlay: How to Bet Horses Like a Pro
Leading trainers and jockeys share their handicapping secrets
Bill Heller
ISBN 0-933893-86-8
228 pages—paper—$9.95

Harness Overlays: Beat the Favorite
We'll show you how
Bill Heller
ISBN 0-929387-97-X
139 pages—paper—$12.00

Woulda, Coulda, Shoulda
"Best introduction to horse racing ever written"—*Thoroughbred Times*
Dave Feldman with Frank Sugano
ISBN 0-933893-02-3
281 pages—paper—$9.95

Bonus Books, Inc., 160 East Illinois Street, Chicago, Illinois 60611

TOLL-FREE: 800 · 225 · 3775   FAX: 312 · 467 · 9271